TRANSACTIONS

of the

American Philosophical Society

Held at Philadelphia for Promoting Useful Knowledge

VOLUME 81, Part 1

Philip the Fair
and the
Ecclesiastical Assemblies
of 1294–1295

JEFFREY H. DENTON

Professor of Medieval History, University of Manchester

THE AMERICAN PHILOSOPHICAL SOCIETY

Independence Square, Philadelphia

1991

Library of Congress Catalog
Card Number-90-56108
International Standard Book Number 0-87169-811-0
US ISSN 0065-9746

CONTENTS

PREFACE

This investigation marks the beginning of a series of studies which have two main aims: a re-assessment of the position of the French Church vis-à-vis the Crown and the Papacy at the turn of the thirteenth century, and a new selection and new edition of the texts concerning the famous clash between Philip the Fair and Boniface VIII, many of which were last edited in 1655 by Pierre Dupuy in his *Histoire du Différend d'entre le Pape Boniface VIII et Phillipe le Bel roy de France*. Although Dupuy's collection of evidence is copious, it has significant gaps. None of the material relating to the ecclesiastical assemblies of 1294-5, essential for an understanding of the opening of the conflict between Philip and Boniface, is to be found there. The archival work on which the following is based could not have been undertaken without the support of the British Academy: successive grants have assisted with expenses and I was privileged to hold a British Academy Readership from 1983 to 1986 when essential preparatory research was completed. I owe a debt of gratitude to many archivists and librarians in the Archives Nationales and Bibliothèque Nationale in Paris, the Archives Départementales at Angers and Evreux, and the Stadsbibliotheek at Bruges, without whose assistance the editions of texts in the appendices would not have been possible. I am also very grateful to M. Jean-Loup Lemaitre and Mlle Elizabeth Lalou, who gave me invaluable assistance with the reading of some of the manuscripts in the Archives Nationales and with the identification of place-names.

PHILIP THE FAIR AND THE ECCLESIASTICAL ASSEMBLIES OF 1294-1295

The time is ripe for a new analysis of the sources concerning the clash between Philip the Fair and Boniface VIII. The first stages of this famous dispute were very largely determined by events which occurred during the years immediately preceding Boniface's election as pope on 24 December 1294. One of these events was the controversial resignation of his predecessor, Celestine V. But other developments were also important. The king's financial demands upon the clergy, made at a series of ecclesiastical councils held throughout the realm, merit close attention, for the repercussions of the king's actions in 1294 were far-reaching. And there is a second compelling reason for studying in detail these demands. Any attempt to study the constitutional and political position of the French clergy during the critical years at the turn of the thirteenth century must include an assessment of the ecclesiastical assemblies at which many clerical decisions were taken and through which the clerical voice was being heard. Although much progress has been made in recent years in the sorting and listing of materials relating to French diocesan synods,[1] there has been no comparable sifting of the sources for the provincial councils. The work of diocesan and provincial assemblies to some extent overlapped, but the latter certainly need special and separate treatment. Partly no doubt because the evidence is piecemeal and scattered, French ecclesiastical councils have not enjoyed the attentions of a Powicke and Cheney, whose *magnum opus*

---

[1] See Odette PONTAL, Les statuts synodaux (Typologie des sources du Moyen Age occidental, ed. L.Genicot, fasc. 11, 1975) and André ARTONNE, Louis GUIZARD and Odette PONTAL, Répertoire des statuts synodaux des diocèses de l'ancienne France du XIIIe à la fin du XVIIIe siècle, 2nd edn, Paris, 1969. An important bibliographical guide to primary and secondary sources relating to ecclesiastical councils is provided by Jacobus Theodorus SAWICKI, Bibliographia synodorum particularium (Monumenta iuris canonici, C: subsidia, 2), Vatican, 1967. And see now Joseph AVRIL, L'évolution du synode diocésain, principalement dans la France du Nord du Xe au XIIIe siècle, in Proceedings of the seventh international congress of medieval canon law, ed. Peter LINEHAN, Vatican, 1988, pp. 305-25, and the bibliographies in Les conciles de la province de Tours XIIIe-XVe siècles, ed. Joseph AVRIL, Centre National de la Recherche Scientifique, Paris, 1987.

concerning English ecclesiastical councils, while planned as a revision of the work of Wilkins published in 1737, turned out to be an undertaking of quite new dimensions.[2]

There has been, it is true, some recent work on French conciliar legislation and on councils in a few of the French provinces.[3] Notably, the provincial councils of the province of Tours have now been analysed in detail by Joseph Avril.[4] Yet, for the primary sources relating to French provincial councils other than those of Tours we must still rely upon the large collections of conciliar material of the seventeenth and eighteenth centuries.[5] These ambitious collections can, however, provide only a

---

[2]See Concilia Magnae Britannicae et Hiberniae, ed. David WILKINS (4 vols, 1737) and Councils & synods and other documents relating to the English Church, II 1205-1313, ed. Frederick M.POWICKE and Christopher R.CHENEY, Oxford, 2 parts, 1964.

[3]See Gabriel LE BRAS, Charles LEFEBVRE and Jacqueline RAMBAUD, L'âge classique 1140-1378: sources et théorie du droit (Histoire du droit et des institutions de l'église en occident, ed. Gabriel LE BRAS, 7, Paris, 1965), pp. 191-4 and Jean GAUDEMET, Aspects de la législation conciliaires française au XIIIe siècle, in Revue de droit canonique, 9, 1959, pp. 319-34 (reprinted in Jean GAUDEMET, La formation du droit canonique médiéval, London, 1980). And see Raymonde FOREVILLE, The synod of the province of Rouen in the eleventh and twelfth centuries, in Church and government in the middle ages: essays presented to C.R.Cheney, ed. Christopher N.L.BROOKE et al., Cambridge, 1976, pp. 19-39; eadem, Les statuts synodaux et le renouveau pastoral du XIIIe siècle dans le midi de la France, in Cahiers de Fanjeaux, 6, 1971, pp. 119-50; Richard KAY, The making of statutes in French provincial councils 1049-1305, PhD thesis, Wisconsin, 1959; idem, An episcopal petition from the province of Rouen, 1281, in Church history, 34, 1965, 294-305; idem, Mansi and Rouen: a critique of the conciliar collections, in Catholic historical review, 52, 1966, pp. 155-85; for the provincial councils of Narbonne see Eric W.KEMP, Counsel and consent, London, 1961, pp. 36-9, 48-56; and for Bourges see L. DE LACGER, La primatie et le pouvoir métropolitain de l'archevêque de Bourges au XIIIe siècle, in Revue d'histoire ecclésiastique, 26, 1930, pp. 283-94.

[4]See Conciles de Tours, ed AVRIL (above n. 1) and below Appendix D.

[5]The work of Jacques SIRMOND (Concilia antiqua Galliae, 3 vols, Paris, 1629), covering only the period 314-987, was extended in the Collectio regia ordered by Richelieu (Conciliorum omnium generalium et provincialium collectio regia, 37 vols, Paris, 1644). Even so, the references to provincial councils in this work are very few indeed; only one council held in France during Philip IV's reign is included and it is spurious: vol. 28, p. 688, a council supposedly held at Lyons in 1297 with Boniface VIII presiding. This fictitious council can be traced back to Polydore VERGIL (see Angliae historiae libri vigintisex, Basle, 1553, p. 337) and Gilbertus GENEBRARDUS (see Chronographiae, Lyons, 1609, p. 661). Collections which were more detailed and more reliable - though very far from complete - soon followed: see Philippe LABBE and Gabriel COSSART, Sacrosancta concilia ad regiam editionem exacta, 17 vols., Paris, 1671-2; Jean HARDOUIN, Acta conciliorum, 12 vols., Paris, 1714-15; Niccolo COLETI, Sacrosancta concilia ad regiam editionem exacta, 23 vols., Venice, 1728-33; and Giovanni Domenico MANSI, Sacrorum conciliorum nova et amplissima collectio, 31 vols., Florence, 1759-98; with the very useful additions of Edmund MARTENE and Ursin DURAND, Thesaurus novus anecdotorum, 5 vols., Paris, 1717. These were the basic sources for the work of HEFELE, revised by LECLERCQ: Histoire des conciles d'après les documents originaux, ed. Charles-Joseph

starting-point to our enquiry. They comprise, above all, editions of ecclesiastical statutes and are concerned scarcely at all with wider aspects of the composition and functions of provincial councils. Massive though the collections are, they include only a small proportion of the surviving texts and they provide few indications of the importance of ecclesiastical assemblies for an understanding of the relations of the clergy with the secular powers. As Gaudemet has commented they do not claim to include all councils and too often they leave one in ignorance about everything concerning the manner of holding an assembly, who presided, the numbers and the names of those who attended, or the role of any envoys from the pope or from secular leaders.[6] The large body of material edited below concerning the assemblies which met in 1294-5 at the request of the king - in some cases, quite clearly at the mandate of the king - serves to demonstrate the need for a comprehensive edition of the texts relating to French ecclesiastical assemblies, in order to provide a secure basis for the study of the influence and standing of the French Church in its relations both with the Papacy and with the Crown.

The Anglo-French hostilities, which caused the imposition of unusually heavy royal taxation upon the clergy, had begun with a battle off the coast of Brittany in May 1293 between a fleet of the Cinque Ports and a Norman fleet, followed by a retaliatory attack by Philip the Fair upon Gascony.[7] In May 1294 Philip passed a sentence of forfeiture on the duchy of Gascony. The ensuing Anglo-French war proved to be one of the most critical factors affecting papal relations with the West for virtually the whole of Boniface VIII's period of office. Open hostilities between England and her allies and France and her allies were in fact few and far between; but the policies which stemmed from the outbreak of war were to result in conflicts which undermined papal authority in the West. In England and in France the forfeiture of Gascony led immediately in 1294 to clerical taxation which was quite exceptional not only in its scale but also in the procedures adopted for its implementation. While the unprecedented demands by Edward I for financial support from the English Church have been studied in some detail,[8] the contemporary demands by Philip the Fair upon the French

---

HEFELE, trans. and re-ed. Henri LECLERCQ, 8 vols in 16, Paris, 1907-21.

[6]GAUDEMET (see n. 3), p. 320n.

[7]See Jeffrey H.DENTON, Robert Winchelsey and the crown 1294-1313, Cambridge, 1970, p. 60 and Michael PRESTWICH, Edward I, London, 1988, pp. 376-80.

[8]See DENTON, pp. 60-80, H.S.DEIGHTON, Clerical taxation by consent 1279-1301, English Historical Review, 68, 1953, pp. 171-5 and POWICKE and CHENEY (see n. 2), pp. 1125-34.

Church have been given only cursory treatment.[9] Yet, in France as in England, the king's critical need of resources put his relations with the Church to the test.

The clergy, both French and English, had become accustomed to being taxed by papal mandate.[10] The money collected by papal decree had been passing into the royal treasuries and the path had thus been opened up for the possibility of direct royal taxation. In England proceeds from the most recent papal tax conceded in 1291 (a sexennial tenth to support the king's projected crusade) were seized by Edward in 1294 and the papal tax quickly replaced by an enormous royal tax of a half of the clergy's income, imposed by the king at an assembly of the clergy of the whole realm. This clerical assembly of September 1294 was summoned directly by the king and controlled by him. Developments in France were similar, and study of them must begin with the papal tenths on which the royal tax was to be modelled.

Papal tenths had been levied on the French clergy directly to aid the policies of the Crown whether planning a crusade to the Holy Land or in promoting the war against Aragon: a triennial tenth granted in 1274, a quadrennial tenth in 1284 and a triennial tenth in 1289.[11] The last of these was conceded by Nicholas IV in bulls dated 31 May 1289.[12] Although

---

[9]See Edgard BOUTARIC, La France sous Philippe le Bel, Paris, 1861, pp. 280-3 (expanded upon by Joseph R.STRAYER, Consent to taxation under Philip the Fair, pp. 25-9, in Joseph R.STRAYER and Charles H.TAYLOR, Studies in early French taxation, Cambridge Massachusetts, 1939) and Joseph R.STRAYER, The reign of Philip the Fair, Princeton, 1980, pp. 149-53.

[10]For the papal tenths collected in France during the thirteenth century see especially Adolphe VUITRY, Etudes sur le régime financier de la France, nouv. sér. 1, Paris, 1883, pp. 170-8, Louis BOURGAIN, Contribution du clergé à l'impôt sous la monarchie française, in Revue des questions historiques, nouv. sér. 4, 1890, pp. 64-76, Emile CHENON, Histoire générale du droit français public et privé, Paris, 1926, 1, pp. 911-16, Gabriel LE BRAS, L'immunité réelle: étude sur la formation de la théorie canonique de la participation de l'église aux charges de l'état et sur son application dans la monarchie française au XIIIe siècle, Rennes, 1920, pp. 125-51, and Ursmer BERLIERE, Les décimes pontificales dans les anciens diocèses belges aux XIIIe et XIVe siècles, in Académie royale de Belgique, Bulletins de la classe des lettres et des sciences morales et politiques, 5th series 11, 1925, pp. 99-125. It is a pity that the work of Gerbaux more than a century ago was never developed into a detailed published study of Franco-papal taxation in the thirteenth century: see Fernand GERBAUX, Les décimes ecclésiastiques au XIIIe, in Positions des thèses de l'Ecole des Chartes, 1881, Paris, pp. 23-9.

[11]VUITRY (see n. 10), pp. 171-2, BOUTARIC (see n. 9), p. 279 and Charles-Victor LANGLOIS, Le règne de Philippe le Hardi, Paris, 1887, p. 353.

[12]Les registres de Nicolas IV (1288-92), ed. Ernest LANGLOIS, Bibliothèque des écoles françaises d'Athènes et de Rome, 2 vols, 1905, nos. 615, 991-1009, Les actes pontificaux originaux des Archives Nationales de Paris, 2 (1261-1304), ed. Bernard BARBICHE, Vatican City, 1978, nos. 1817, 1825-36, 1842-3, 1845 and August POTTHAST (ed), Regesta pontificum Romanorum 1198-1304, 2 vols, Berlin, 1874-5, nos. 22817, 22971.

granted at the request of the French Crown and for its benefit, these were certainly papal rather than royal taxes: all matters concerning their assessment and collection were directly authorised by the pope. In 1289 it was the archbishop of Rouen and the bishop of Auxerre who were appointed as the papal deputies charged with the execution of the papal mandates relating to the new triennial tenth. Even so, the problems which quickly emerged about both the method and the extent of the collection of this tax are an indication of the already uneasy collaboration of pope and king in the matter of clerical taxation. On 30 June 1289 the pope specifically decreed that no layman and no-one from the royal household ('de familia regis'), even if a clerk, was to be involved in the business of the tenth.[13] But the degree of the Crown's involvement in the collection of the tax is revealed in letters of 10 July 1290. On that date both the king and the papal deputies wrote in almost identical terms to the collectors of the tax in the province of Bourges.[14] The collectors, referred to by the king as *his* collectors, were ordered to refuse no longer to assign the proceeds from the tenth to Florentine merchants and to the king's valet Biche Guidi, who was at the beginning of his influential career as a royal financial agent and adviser. As we might have expected, it is clear that the king and the papal deputies were to some extent working together.

The whole question of the collection of papal tenths to aid the king's policies against Aragon came under particular strain in the early 1290s. The 1289 triennial tenth was the last papal tenth granted to the French Crown which extended to many dioceses of the old Middle Kingdom. The attempt to collect the tenth from imperial dioceses, in territories over which Philip was attempting to extend his protection, caused strong opposition.[15] The papal claim was that the tenth was for the protection of the Church against its enemies rather than to supply the needs of the French Crown. In February 1290 the pope ordered the archbishop of Rouen and the bishop of Auxerre to compel the clergy of the provinces of Lyons, Vienne and Besançon and of the dioceses of Cambrai, Liège, Metz, Toul and Verdun to pay the tax. But the protests from the clergy of these regions, and indeed from German princes and magnates and from King Rudolf of Hapsburg, were not easily silenced. Pope Nicholas issued a further order to his deputies in December 1291, but it may be that the tax proved difficult to collect in some of those areas which were regarded as outside the French realm. An

---

[13]Reg. Nic. (see n. 12), no. 1008, and Les actes pontificaux (see n. 12), no. 1843.

[14]BN Doat 11, fos. 153v-156r (copies of letters once in the archive of the bishop of Albi).

[15]See Reg. Nic. (see n. 12), nos. 2114, 4312, 6316, Les actes pontificaux (see n. 12), nos. 1860, 1912, Regesta imperii, ed. Johann F.BOHMER, 6 part 1, reprinted Hildesheim, 1969, pp. 506-7, Fritz KERN, Die Anfänge der französischen Ausdehnungspolitik bis zum Jahr 1308, Tübingen, 1910, p. 133, and STRAYER, Philip the Fair (see n. 9), pp. 315-16, 350-1, 365.

account for the tax - and it is indeed a *compotus* rather than a *valor* - includes sums for three years from the diocese of Cambrai but only for two years from the dioceses of Liège, Toul and Verdun and nothing at all (except from the clergy exempt from episcopal authority) from the diocese of Metz, and nothing also from the dioceses of Valence et Die and Viviers (province of Vienne) and Basle (province of Besançon).[16] In addition, the absence of sums for the second term of the second year and for the third year from the dioceses of the provinces of Narbonne and Auch suggests that the problems of collection may have spread to regions of southern France. But the papal legates at work in France in 1290 had certainly shown a continuing commitment to the collection of the tenths,[17] and Mignon's inventory of accounts in fact suggests a more consistent rate of collection across the realm as well as 'in partibus Imperii', even though, as was generally the case, arrears continued to be accounted for well after 1292.[18] If there was more than usual hesitancy in making final payments the reason could well have been that the pope's own position in relation to crusading tenths changed dramatically in the course of 1291.

Following the fall of Acre in May, Pope Nicholas, in bulls issued on 1 August 1291, exhorted all Christians to take the cross and thus follow the lead of Edward I of England, who planned to set out for the Holy Land in 1293.[19] On 18 August the pope summoned ecclesiastical councils to be held throughout the West to discuss the business of the Holy Land and to send him conclusions and suggestions.[20] Provincial councils summoned directly by the pope were most unusual, though Alexander IV had followed the same procedure in 1261.[21] Councils probably met in all the provinces of France, early in 1292.[22] We have certain knowledge of the following: the

---

[16]Recueil des historiens des Gaules et de la France, ed. Martin BOUQUET et al, Paris, 1783-1904, 21, pp. 546-56.

[17]See the terms of the Treaty of Senlis, August 1290: Georges DIGARD, Philippe le Bel et le saint-siège de 1285 à 1304, Paris, 1936, 1, p. 109 and 2, p. 279.

[18]Inventaire d'anciens comptes royaux dressé par Robert Mignon sous le règne de Philippe de Valois, ed Charles-Victor LANGLOIS (Recueil des historiens de la France, Documents financiers 1, Paris, 1899), pp. 95-8.

[19]Reg. Nic. (see n. 12), nos. 6800-5 and POTTHAST (see n. 12), nos. 23756-63.

[20]Reg. Nic., nos. 6791-9 and POTTHAST, nos. 23783, 23786-7, 23793. I have benefited greatly from an account of these councils in Barrie J.COOK, The transmission of knowledge about the Holy Land through Europe 1271-1314, Manchester PhD, 1985, pp. 142-72.

[21]See HEFELE-LECLERCQ (see n. 5), 6 part 1, pp. 95, 97, 99 and POWICKE and CHENEY (see n. 2), p. 661.

[22]Chronique latine de Guillaume de Nangis, ed. Hercule GERAUD, 2 vols, Paris, 1843, 1, p. 279, and Les grandes chroniques de France, ed. Jules VIARD, 10 vols, Paris, 1920-53, 8, p. 146.

provincial council of Sens met at Paris on 9 January, as witnessed by an abbreviated version of its response and by the reply to the pope of the prelates of the province;[23] the council of Rheims was held at Compiègne on 20 January, as we know from the inclusion of the summons and conclusions in the chronicle of John of Thielrode who attended it;[24] a memorandum in the register of Guillaume le Maire, bishop of Angers, records that the council of Tours met at Angers from 26 to 30 January;[25] and undated sets of conclusions from the councils of Lyons and Arles are included in the chronicle of Bartholomew Cotton.[26] Of these councils only the one at Angers is listed in Hefele-Leclercq;[27] and among all the accounts of Philip's reign it is only Digard's which takes note, in brief, of their importance.[28] One feature of the papally-summoned councils was the inclusion within them of the exempt clergy, normally, of course, excluded by reason of their exemption from provincial councils summoned solely by the authority of archbishops. This, as we shall see, will be a matter of some significance in respect of the councils soon to be summoned at the king's request. In his great concern for the future of the Holy Land the pope was clearly very eager to gain the support of Philip the Fair: on 23 August 1291 he asked Philip to send naval assistance immediately to the East, and on the following day he reminded Philip that his father had taken the cross and had received a tenth for the purpose of going on crusade and he asked that if he did not himself take the cross he should at any rate assign the proceeds of the earlier crusading tenth granted in 1274 - as, indeed, he had already requested the previous year - to the papal nominees, now the bishops of Paris and Spoleto.[29]

---

[23]Johannis de Thilrode chronicon, ed. Johann HELLER, Monumenta Germaniae historica, scriptorum, 25, 1880, pp. 581-2 and DIGARD (see n. 17), 2, pp. 281-3.

[24]Johannis de Thilrode chronicon, pp. 580-1, and see the note in Annales Blandienses, ed. Ludwig BETHMANN, MGH, scriptorum, 5, 1844, p. 34.

[25]Livre de Guillaume le Maire, ed. Célestin PORT, in Mélanges historiques: choix de documents (Collection de documents inédits sur l'histoire de France, 5 vols, Paris, 1873-86), 2, pp. 274-5.

[26]Bartholomaei de Cotton monachi Norwicensis Historia Anglicana, ed. Henry R.LUARD, Rolls Series, 1859, pp. 210-15.

[27]HEFELE-LECLERCQ (see n. 5), 6 part 1, p. 327.

[28]DIGARD (see n. 17),1, pp. 139-40; but see also the additions to HEFELE-LECLERCQ in Heinrich FINKE, Konzilienstudien zur Geschichte des 13 Jahrhunderts, Münster, 1891, pp. 103-5.

[29]Reg. Nic. (see n. 12), nos. 6778-9, POTTHAST (see n. 12), nos. 23246, 23794 and BARBICHE (see n. 12), nos. 1900-1. Edward I of England had been trying, unsuccessfully, to lay claim to the proceeds of earlier crusading tenths collected from the clergy of France, Castile and Germany, and from the Cistercian order: Thomas RYMER, Foedera conventiones litterae,

The surviving conclusions of the clergy meeting in the provinces of Sens, Tours, Lyons and Arles provide important evidence of ecclesiastical attitudes in France in 1291-2. It is interesting, in the first place, that those in attendance appear to have been well aware of decisions that had been reached in other assemblies: a short version of the response to be made to the pope from the province of Sens survives alongside the response from Rheims in John of Thielrode's chronicle and the responses from the provinces of Lyons and Arles survive in Cotton's chronicle with the evidence relating to the provincial council at Canterbury. Each assembly was apparently influenced by others and there was an effective network of communication. It was clearly not at all easy for the French clergy to present a decisive and unambiguous response to the pope's call for a crusade, for they had to balance the urgent needs of Christendom with all the practical problems which support for a crusade would bring. The clergy's uncertainty is brought out by the indications of a degree of deference towards the pope: if the responses are not found adequate the pope should put it down to the clergy's lack of wisdom (Sens) or insufficiency (Lyons) and, more generally, the shortness of time which they had been given to reply. The last section of the conclusions arrived at in the council of Rheims, which seems to be a section addressed by the monks to the bishops of the council, is a plea for forgiveness for ignorance, arising not only from the brevity of their deliberations but also from their complete lack of expertise in military matters.

While there are differences of emphasis in the responses certain points are repeatedly stressed: peace in the West was a necessary pre-condition for a crusade; the election of a new king of the Romans who could defend the Christian faith should take place quickly; the Hospitallers and the Templars, and indeed other military orders, should be united, if it could be done without scandal, and their goods used for the recovery and the retention of the Holy Land; and the French clergy would pay a subsidy for the crusade, despite the fact that they were so burdened that they could hardly breathe (Sens) and so ground down that recovery was scarcely possible (Lyons), as

London, 1816-30, 1 part 2, p. 743, Reg. Nic., no. 6857 and POTTHAST, no. 23921. In response to a papal *monitio*, which caused some animosity against the pope's agent, Reinerius de Vichio, canon of Lichfield, the abbots of Cîteaux and Clairvaux made a formal declaration in Paris on 9 April 1292 that they were doing all in their power to obey the papal orders concerning the proceeds of the earlier tenth (specifically referred to as the tenth granted to Gregory X at the Council of Lyons): Bruges, Stadsbibliotheek MS 481, fos. 211r-214r (item 359), printed in Codex Dunensis, ed. J.B.M.C. KERVYN DE LETTENHOVE, Brussels, 1875, no. 117. Kervyn de Lettenhove completely misinterpreted this document as an appeal against the usurpations of Philip IV: KERVYN DE LETTENHOVE, Etudes sur l'histoire du XIIIe siècle, in Patrologiae ... Latina, ed. J.P.MIGNE, 185, cols. 1837-8 (reprinted from Mémoires de l'académie royale des sciences, des lettres, et des beaux arts de Belgique, 28, 1954, pp. 8-9).

long, that is, as the whole of Christendom contributed, laity as well as clergy - and even the Jews (Sens).

The churchmen of France felt in general that a great deal needed to be done before a crusade to the East was a practical proposition. Great expense and labour must be avoided unless it was clear that there would be a fruitful outcome. (Rheims) But there was also a common belief that French military aid was essential. Philip should be asked if he or someone else of royal blood would take up the cross, for by his leadership the French and other peoples would rise up with greater confidence against the enemies of the faith. (Rheims) Following universal prayers and the establishment of peace, and at the advice of the king, if he himself did not wish to shoulder the burden, a powerful and persuasive leader should be appointed to lead a French army. (Lyons)

The short version of the discussion in the Sens council at Paris also stated that the king of France or some other Frenchman should lead the crusading army. But it is very striking that this version of the discussion at Paris differs greatly from the much longer letter addressed to the pope, from the archbishop of Sens, the bishops of Paris, Orléans, Auxerre, Meaux, Troyes and Nevers (only the bishop of Chartres was absent) the abbots of St-Denis, St-Germain-des-Prés and St-Victor, and the whole ecclesiastical council. This letter, drawn up in all probability after the discussion had taken place, bears all the marks of royal influence. Here there are much firmer propositions about policies which should be pursued before the launching of a crusade to the Holy Land. For example, a truce should be established between the Genoese, the Pisans and the Venetians so that their maritime skills could be used to aid the wars of the kings of France and Sicily and to defend the island of Cyprus, and, since the co-operation of the Greeks was so beneficial for access to the Holy Land, they should be brought back to obedience to the Roman see. These propositions must have been understood as largely unattainable, in the short term at least. What could be achieved, however, was a successful outcome to the crusade against the Aragonese, and this was still a matter of great concern. A peace treaty had been concluded with Alphonse of Aragon at Tarascon in February 1291,[30] but peace had been threatened by the sudden death of Alphonse in June and the succession to the throne of his brother James whose interests in Sicily had been abandoned at Tarascon. The French now felt threatened by James and 'his accomplices', and the bishops stressed the need for peace between James and the kings of France and Sicily and suggested that if James would not turn his back upon rebellion then the whole of Christendom should turn against him.

---

[30]BOUTARIC (see n. 9), p. 382 and Frederick M.POWICKE, The thirteenth century, 2nd edn, Oxford, 1962, pp. 261-3.

With the prelates of the Sens province at least, surely under the close influence of the Crown, the crusade against Aragon remained a priority.

Despite the implications of this letter from the province of Sens the French clergy in their provincial councils certainly gave some heartfelt support, at any rate in principle, to the pope's crusading plans. Their king had other schemes and was clearly not greatly moved by the papal arguments of *urgens necessitas*. His own interests lay elsewhere and certainly not in the direction of aiding a crusade to which Edward I of England was committed. He had sent his nuncios, including the bishop-elect of Carcassonne, Pierre de la Chapelle, to ask the pope that a further tenth be granted, for six years, from the clergy of the French realm to aid his war against Aragon and that a crusade be preached in France against the Aragonese. This took no account of the change in papal policy and the king's requests had naturally been refused, in a papal letter dated 13 December 1291.[31] However we may judge previous Franco-papal co-operation in the *negotium Aragonie*, the aims of king and pope had certainly now diverged. In addition, the prospect of success for the renewed attempt to organise the urgently required crusade to the Holy Land was gravely weakened by Nicholas IV's death on 4 April 1292, by which time the replies from the provincial councils can scarcely have been gathered in. The long papal vacancy which followed spelt disaster not only for the crusade but also for papal control over ecclesiastical tenths.

The terms for the final payments of the 1289 triennial tenth were Christmas 1291 and 24 June 1292. Clerical tenths had certainly become a major item of royal income. While no precise calculations of the Crown's total revenue are possible, a tenth was probably the equivalent of little short of a half of the Crown's annual revenue.[32] The 1289 tenth was worth, without taking into account delays in payment, in excess of 265,000 *livres tournois* each year,[33] though a total of 200,000 *livres tournois* for the three years was claimed by the pope.[34] The king of France, like the king of England, had come to rely very heavily on extraordinary taxation. But the regular sums which the French clergy had been paying from the beginning of the reign were drying up in 1292, and between the spring of 1292 and the

---

[31] Reg. Nic., no. 6849, POTTHAST, no. 23874 and BARBICHE, no. 1910.

[32] See Joseph R.STRAYER, The costs and profits of war: the Anglo-French conflict of 1294-1303, in The medieval city, ed. Harry A.MISKIMIN, New Haven & London, 1977, p. 273 and Jean FAVIER, Philippe le Bel, Paris, 1978, p. 186.

[33] See STRAYER, Philip the Fair (see n. 9), pp. 146-7 and the totals in Recueil des historiens (see n. 16), XXI, pp. 556-7, which are incomplete (for the separate payments from the Cistercians see ibid, pp. 531-2 and Essai de restitution des plus anciens mémoriaux de la chambre des comptes de Paris, ed. Joseph PETIT, Université de Paris, Bibliothèque de la Faculté des Lettres, 7, 1899, no. 332, and see above p. 6 & n. 18).

[34] BARBICHE (see n. 12), nos. 1825, 1898 and Reg. Nic. (see n. 12), nos. 1004, 7379.

summer of 1294 there was no pope in office to be petitioned for a further grant. Without a papal mandate there could not be - or rather there had never been - a grant from clerical income.

Occasionally prelates, chapters and abbeys had granted subsidies to the king at times of special need: Le Bras noted examples from 1224, 1242 and 1266.[35] But these aids had been, there can be little doubt, grants from ecclesiastical estates, that is from temporalities, and not, like the papal tenths, from the totality of ecclesiastical income, temporal or spiritual, whether of the lower clergy or of the higher clergy. It was accepted in canon law that lands granted to the Church, though not the lands on which a church was founded, could continue to bear traditional secular burdens.[36] There is no doubt, however, that all previous ecclesiastical subsidies for the Crown, of whatever kind, had been completely overshadowed in the thirteenth century by the papal tenths. The clergy guarded their freedom from impositions by secular princes. A *quodlibet*, delivered in 1282 by a secular master in theology at Paris, Berthaud de Saint-Denys, is precise on the matter. It should be noted immediately that it seems clear that Berthaud, who became bishop of Orléans in 1300, was to give support to the king in the final stage of his conflict with Boniface VIII;[37] nonetheless, in 1282 he was stressing clerical rights. About extraordinary taxation he noted that there were some who believed that the clergy were bound to contribute to royal taxation when lay contributions were insufficient. But he declared his belief that the king had no such right, though the clergy could indeed voluntarily offer financial assistance at a time of emergency.[38] The matter was a question of vital contemporary debate and the development of the doctrine of necessity, within the framework of the wider discussion of what constituted justifiable taxation,[39] gave some moral authority, if not legal right, to secular leaders in looking to their churchmen for financial support. Some scholars went further than Berthaud de Saint-Denys. In 1285-6 the

---

[35]LE BRAS (above n. 10), pp. 130-1.

[36]Extra, 3, 39, 1 (Corpus iuris canonici, ed. Emile FRIEDBERG, Leipzig, 1879-81, 2, p. 622) and Jean LECLERCQ, Deux questions de Berthaud de Saint-Denys sur l'exemption fiscale du clergé, in Etudes d'histoire du droit canonique, dédiées à Gabriel le Bras, Paris, 1965, 1, p. 612.

[37]Palémon GLORIEUX, Répertoire des maîtres en théologie de Paris au XIIIe siècle, Paris, 1933, 1, p. 393.

[38]LECLERCQ (see n. 36), p. 612. The decretal referred to in this context is surely not 'Novimus' (Extra, 5, 40, 27), but rather 'Non minus' (Extra, 3, 49, 4: FRIEDBERG (above n. 36), 2, pp. 654-5).

[39]DENTON (above n. 7), p. 97, Jeffrey H. DENTON and John P. DOOLEY, Representatives of the lower clergy in parliament 1295-1340, London, 1987, p. 5 and Elizabeth A.R. BROWN, Taxation and morality in the thirteenth and fourteenth centuries: conscience and political power and the kings of France, in: French historical studies, 8, 1973-4, 1-28.

Franciscan theologian Richard de Mediavilla, in his second *quodlibet*, while supporting the principles of ecclesiastical immunity, argued that it was just for the clergy to contribute to necessary expenses from which they gained particular advantages.[40] Despite these moderating voices, everything points to a determination on the part of the clergy to defend their right of consent to secular taxation. The pope's right to tax the clergy was by mandate. Not so the king's.

The doctrine of necessity sought, at the very least, to free secular leaders, at times of emergency, from the obligation to seek a papal licence before taxing the clergy. This was not the same as freedom from the obligation to seek clerical consent. After stressing the voluntary nature of clerical financial aids Berthaud de Saint-Denys had noted, as indeed canon law in fact dictated, that papal permission should first be sought. But the principle of papal control of all clerical taxation, set down at the Third and Fourth Lateran Councils,[41] had not yet been put fully to the test: this was to happen after it received its most forceful expression in 'Clericis laicos' of 1296. In the 1280s clerical consent and papal permission could be linked together in arguments concerned with clerical as opposed to lay rights, with little thought that they could be regarded as separate and separable matters.

Further evidence that the clergy at this time were eager to defend themselves from secular financial demands is not difficult to find. For example, on 11 July 1283 proctors of the cathedral churches of the province of Rheims met together at St-Quentin and drew up a statement in defence of the 'liberty and immunity' of their churches.[42] It had been brought to the notice of the cathedral churches of the provinces of Rheims and Sens that many leading men at the side of the king ('nonnulli magnates de latere illustrissimi domini regis') were pressing that they should pay a subsidy to the king, Philip III. This was just before the papal grant of a quadrennial tenth to Philip.[43] The representatives of the cathedral churches of Rheims noted that no similar subsidy for the king could be recalled. While they had no wish to offend the king, they agreed, lest they harm their consciences and lest the Gallican Church be harmed, that they should maintain the liberty and immunity which the Gallican Church had always enjoyed. Clearly the clerical right of freedom from secular taxation would be vigorously defended.

---

[40]Edgar HOCEDEZ, Richard de Middletown sa vie ses oeuvres sa doctrine, Louvain & Paris, 1925, pp. 231, 417, 440, and see Palémon GLORIEUX, La littérature quodlibétique de 1260 à 1320, 2 vols., Paris, 1925-35, 1, pp. 267-73, and DIGARD (see n. 17), 1, p. 259.

[41]See DENTON (above n. 7), p. 90.

[42]Thomas DUCHET & Arthur GIRY, Cartulaires de l'église de Thérouane, St Omer, 1881, pp. 203-5.

[43]LANGLOIS, Philippe le Hardi (above n. 11), pp. 146-8.

The right was certainly threatened again, and far more dramatically, by the king's demands in 1294.

The king's financial needs following the outbreak of Anglo-French hostilities in 1293 certainly reached a new peak. He required the support of his Church and he knew that his Church had the wherewithal to support him. Papal taxation of the clergy on behalf of the king had produced an expectation of financial subsidies from clerical income, and the Crown had already been closely involved in the collection of papal tenths. There was no pope to petition for new papal tenths between April 1292 and July 1294. Even if there had been, Franco-papal co-operation had broken down, and the war with England could hardly in any case have been raised to the status of a crusade. Indeed, Philip had turned his hostilities towards the very man on whom the papacy had been relying to lead a new crusade to the East. In their relations with their clergy both kings took advantage of the papal vacancy and of the weak rule of Celestine V (July to December 1294) which followed it.

Philip probably had confidence that the clergy would support him if they accepted the argument of necessity. In 1292, as we have seen, they had found many reasons for avoiding financial commitments to a papal crusade which had little or no chance of success and, just as important in their minds perhaps, one which was not supported by the French king or by the French nobility. They had no desire to turn their backs on the wider needs of Christendom, but there can be little doubt that, despite the fall of Acre, defence of the realm could easily be seen as a far more pressing problem. Yet there was no precedent for direct royal taxation of clerical income: the king would have to move very cautiously in a matter as sensitive as secular encroachment on ecclesiastical resources. Much work needs to be done before we have a clear understanding of the pattern of allegiances among the French bishops during these years,[44] but we know enough to be sure that there was a strong sense of allegiance to the Crown especially in the dioceses of the North. In this regard it is useful to recall a treatise written apparently by Drogo de Altovillari[45] (canon of Rheims from at least 1238) following a legatine council held at Paris by Simon cardinal priest of St Cecilia in 1264.[46] The treatise is a lively defence of clerical freedom from exactions, emphasising the need for a proper procedure of clerical consent to financial

---

[44]I shall return to this crucial question in forthcoming publications.

[45]Pierre VARIN, Archives législatives de la ville de Reims, 2 vols in 4, Paris, 1840-52, 1 part 1 (Coutumes), pp. 448-60. For Drogo (or Dreux de Hautvilliers) see Les registres de Grégoire IX (1227-41), ed. Lucien AUVRAY, Bibliothèque des écoles françaises d'Athènes et de Rome, 3 vols, 1896-1908, no. 4514, B.Hauréau in Histoire littéraire de la France, 32, 1898, pp. 598-606, and Catalogue général des manuscrits des bibliothèques de la France, 32, 1904, pp. 370-98.

[46]HEFELE-LECLERCQ (above n. 5), 6 part 1, p. 119.

subsidies. What is unusual is that this is a reaction not to royal demands but rather to papal demands. 'It is said that we must obey the pope, but the truth is that we must obey him in respect of lawful and honest matters, insofar as they are concerned with the safety of our souls, the articles of faith and the doing of God's will, not however when it is a question of violating and plundering our goods.'[47] Drogo's vigorously argued *libellus* serves to warn us that we must not assume that there had been at all times and in all circumstances a ready acquiescence on the part of the clergy in the collection of papal tenths. Taxation of the clergy was not a simple matter of obedience to the pope and resistance to the king. If need be the clergy were perfectly capable of defending their interests independently of Rome, even in opposition to Rome.

The king's own writs in 1294 explained that, in consultation with his council, he had at first intended to summon to his presence in a single assembly all the bishops and the secular and regular clergy of his realm, exempt and non-exempt, and including the rectors of churches (see below Appendices B1a & d and F1). If this indeed had been the king's intention, and there is no reason to doubt it, he had contemplated the possibility of an ecclesiastical council of quite unprecedented size. And it would have been, too, an unprecedented demonstration of royal control over the French clergy. Philip was probably deterred from proceeding with his scheme by the improbability of gaining the clergy's full acceptance of it. There was not only the problem of the labour and expense of travelling to one council, which would have met no doubt in Paris, - a factor which the king himself stressed as the reason for changing his mind - but there can be no doubt also that many churchmen would have regarded with great alarm the prospect of being summoned directly to meet before the king. The king's court was, after all, a secular court. It is interesting that the king in this remarkable initial plan recognised - or, at least, saw the need to claim that he had recognised - that any attempt to gain a subsidy from the whole clergy required, if it was to have any chance of success, the consent of the whole clergy. This was no easy task in a realm which comprised, for the purposes of this taxation, at least nine ecclesiastical provinces and eighty dioceses. The king, agreeing, we learn, to the wishes of the archbishops of the realm (F1), decided that separate councils should meet in each province. This decision was probably taken shortly before the end of July, not long before the summons issued by the archbishop of Bourges dated 31 July (A1). Whatever the extent of the involvement of the archbishops at this early stage, the ensuing councils, it was quite clear, did not meet in fulfilment of canonical prescriptions. They were certainly at least as much royal as ecclesiastical assemblies. The official of the archbishop of Bourges put it succinctly: they met because of the needs

---

[47]VARIN (above n. 45), p. 450.

of the kingdom and at the request of the lord king (A2). The assemblies of non-exempt clergy of each province (as distinct from the assemblies of exempt clergy and the assemblies of particular monastic orders, which will require separate consideration) were, however, summoned by the respective archbishops.

Indeed, it is difficult to imagine that provincial councils could have been summoned by anyone except the metropolitans. There is direct documentary proof that councils assembled for the provinces of Bourges, Tours, Rheims, Narbonne, Bordeaux, Lyons and Rouen (Appendices A,B,E,F,H,J and L), and evidence relating to taxation returns indicates that councils must also have met for the provinces of Sens and Auch.[48] Yet the only archiepiscopal summons to have survived is that of the archbishop of Bourges (A1). Only one other writ concerning the summons of the non-exempt clergy has come to light and it is a royal writ addressed to the bishop of Uzès (F1). And this writ demonstrates that the king was attempting to exercise, in one province at least, a quite unusual degree of control over the summoning of the clergy. The writ to the bishop of Uzès is a royal mandate requiring the bishop to be present personally at a provincial council, the time and place of which he would learn from the archbishop of Narbonne, and requiring him also, on the king's behalf ('ex parte nostra'), to summon all the clergy of his diocese to be present at the council, the higher clergy in person and the lower clergy by proxy. This mandate is a startling infringement of clerical rights. A mandate ('requirimus presentium tenore mandantes') must be understood as - by its very nature - legally enforceable. It was no gentle request. By what right could the king insist on the attendance of the clergy of a diocese at a provincial council? It is more than likely that the royal summons was in fact superseded by a summons from the archbishop himself. And the king certainly cannot have sent similar writs to all the bishops of his realm. Even so, the existence of the one writ is sufficient to alert us to the unusual nature of the king's constitutional and political intentions in 1294. He was determined that the clergy of his realm would respond to the needs of the realm. His writ to the bishop of Uzès shows that he believed that in an emergency he could, by his own direct authority, order meetings of the clergy so that he could gain their financial assistance. At the same time, we cannot rule out the possibility that the sending of this mandate was connected with the fact that the archbishop of Narbonne, Gilles Aycelin, was a principal royal adviser.[49] Could it have been at the archbishop's own prompting that pressure was put upon the bishop of Uzès in this way?

----

[48]See below, p. 22.

[49]See STRAYER, Philip the Fair (see n. 9), esp. pp. 95-9.

Despite the urgency of the king's demands it is clear that archbishops, or their officials, enjoyed some freedom of action in the procedures that they adopted. The archbishop of Tours issued reforming canons (D1) at the same council at which a grant was conceded to the king. It is interesting that one of the canons was against attacks by laymen upon tithes, for, after all, the subsidy granted to the king was to be paid by the lower clergy largely from their income from tithes. And although at least five of the provincial councils met quite rapidly in the autumn of 1294 (Bourges, Tours, Rheims, Narbonne and Bordeaux), the Lyons council was delayed until 9 February 1295 and the Rouen council seems not to have met until the spring of 1295. There is some evidence, too, of concern about the nature of the assemblies that had been convoked. The assembled clergy of the province of Bourges complained about the terms of their archbishop's summons.(A2) This complaint arose, in part at least, because of the quite unusual degree of clerical representation that had been demanded. All those to be taxed had to be represented. There was no established tradition of full representation of the lower clergy at ecclesiastical assemblies, and certainly not at provincial councils. The lower clergy were being summoned now in France - as also increasingly in England during the latter part of the thirteenth century - for one main reason: to gain their consent to the royal financial demands.[50] It could well be that the clergy of the province of Bourges were worried in 1294 about the whole question of royal taxation of their income. But, in fact, the surviving complaint does not appear to relate directly to the matter of taxation. The problem, it seems, was that the clergy of the whole province, from abbots and archdeacons down to chaplains and perpetual vicars, had been summoned by the archbishop's writ, amounting thereby to a claim that the archbishop had jurisdiction over the clergy in dioceses other than his own. The proper procedure would have been an archiepiscopal writ instructing each bishop of the province to summon the clergy of his diocese. The exact extent of metropolitical authority was often a matter for dispute, and diocesan clergy could, of course, be very sensitive to the claims of archbishops. The clergy who were subjects of the suffragan bishops of the province of Bourges insisted that in this particular instance ('in hoc casu') the archbishop had no power or jurisdiction over them.

Another fear arose at the council of the province of Rheims held at Compiègne. The proctors of the cathedral churches of the province were clearly anxious about the implications for the future of granting a subsidy in the council. They drew up a formal precautionary appeal to Rome, a

---

[50]KEMP (see n. 3), pp. 53, 58, and DENTON & DOOLEY, Representatives (see n. 39), p. 10.

provocatio,[51] against any future action by their archbishop or their bishops which might be prejudicial to them.(E2) Although the cathedral chapters of the province of Rheims appear to have often been on their guard to defend their liberties and rights,[52] it is difficult to think that their proctors would have gone to the trouble of making this appeal to Rome - and the dean and chapter of Laon have gone to the trouble of having the appeal ratified and drawn up in a notarial instrument - if there had not been real concern about the unusual proceedings of the council. There is no doubt whatever that the proctors of the cathedral churches had given their consent to the request for a subsidy, under the conditions specified,(E1) so that it is clear that their fear was not about the royal tax as such but rather about the possibility that their ecclesiastical leaders would act in ways contrary to their will as expressed at the council. In placing their status, their goods and the goods of their churches under papal protection, the deans and chapters of the cathedral churches were seeking to protect themselves from any future incursions by their respective bishops. The recorded fears of the clergy arising from these provincial councils were, thus, that they would mark an increase either in metropolitical authority (as at the Bourges council) or in episcopal authority (as at the Rheims council); and it is interesting that no formal complaints have survived from the provincial councils specifically about being taxed by the king.

In order to obtain the support of the clergy who were not subject to episcopal or archiepiscopal jurisdiction, that is the exempt clergy, the king had to resort to a quite separate procedure. Evidence has survived for assemblies of exempt clergy in the provinces of Narbonne and Bourges (Appendices G and B), and the assumption must be that similar assemblies met in other provinces. The striking fact is that while the exempt clergy were subject directly to Rome, *nullo mediante*, they became quite clearly, for the purpose of this royal taxation, subject more directly to the king's authority than were the non-exempt clergy. Unlike the non-exempt clergy they were summoned by royal mandate and they met before the king's agents; indeed,

---

[51] On *provocationes* see Select cases from the ecclesiastical courts of the province of Canterbury c.1200-1301, ed. Norma ADAMS and Charles DONAHUE, Selden society, 95, 1978-9, intro. p. 62 and n. 6. Further cases are noted in Mark T.BATESON, Papal jurisdiction and courts in England 1272-1327, Manchester PhD, 1987, pp. 187-8, 220, and I am grateful to Dr Bateson for his advice on this matter. For *provocationes* of the English Crown in March and September 1297 against the policies of his archbishop of Canterbury see DENTON (see n. 7), pp. 125, 154-5; and a formulary in Hereford Cathedral, MS P.8.iii contains some forms of *provocationes* (see, for example, fos. 118v-119r 'Provocationes super presumptuosis gravaminibus in electione inferendis').

[52] See above n. 42 and H.NELIS, La 'congrégation' des chapitres cathédraux de la province ecclésiastique de Reims à St-Quentin 1331-1428, in Revue d'histoire ecclésiastique, 25, 1929, esp. pp. 449-53.

their assemblies seem to have been presided over by royal clerks. These assemblies, even more than the provincial councils, were a demonstration of royal *force majeure*.

The king's summons of the exempt clergy of the province of Bourges (B1a) indicates that assemblies of this kind were novel: because, the writ states, the exempt clergy were not in the habit of holding assemblies of this kind or of a similar kind in any given place, and because they could not easily agree on a place to meet, they were required by the king to meet at Clermont-Ferrand on 8 November. Far from being an impediment to royal action, the fact that the exempt clergy were not in the habit of assembling gave the Crown an opportunity to determine both the date and the place of these unusual councils. As we learn from the grants of subsidies (G2 and B2), the exempt of Narbonne met in the king's palace at Béziers and the exempt of Bourges in the house of the Dominicans at Clermont-Ferrand. Even so, the assemblies posed something of a problem for the Crown, for how could the king know exactly who should be summoned? In respect of the province of Bourges a separate summons was required for the diocese of Le Puy (B1d), since the bishop and cathedral chapter of Le Puy were themselves exempt and thus had to be included specifically in the list of those summoned.[53] In order to discover which clergy in addition were exempt, it was necessary to write to the collectors of the previous papal tenths. The seneschal of Beaucaire was thus provided with royal letters (B1b) to be sent to the collectors of the previous papal tenths in order to obtain the names of the exempt of the two dioceses of Mende and Le Puy. The names of the exempt in other dioceses of the province of Bourges were no doubt obtained by other seneschals or *baillis*. And in respect of the province of Narbonne, the seneschals of Toulouse, Carcassonne, Beaucaire and Rouergue were told that the collectors of the tenths knew best who were the exempt in the province.(G1) The procedure worked well, as is clear from the lists of all those present at the two assemblies incorporated into the documents which recorded the grants of the required biennial tenth.

The royal clerk P. de Mauloues, dean of St-Quentin,[54] was apparently in charge of the initial arrangements, at least concerning the assembly for the province of Narbonne.(G1) He sent out the king's summons and instructed the seneschals that they should instruct their *baillis* and *prévots* to cite all the exempt clergy to be at Béziers on 28 October, abbots provosts deans and priors to attend in person and their chapters by proxy. The names of all the clergy summoned were to be forwarded to those about to be sent to act for

---

[53]For the origin of Le Puy's exemption see L. DE LACGER (see n. 3), p. 271.

[54]Probably the same as 'master Petrus de Mauloue' referred to in the accounts of the receivers of the seneschalcy of Toulouse in 1288: Comptes royaux 1285-1314, ed. Robert FAWTIER (Recueil des historiens de la France, Documents financiers III, Paris, 1953-6), 2, no. 16742.

the king in the assembly; and the chosen deputies who duly presided over the assembly were the two royal clerks, Gérard de Maumont, precentor of Bourges, and Pierre de Latilly, canon of Soissons (bishop of Châlons-sur-Marne 1313-28).[55] They both then moved on to Clermont-Ferrand to preside over the second assembly ten days later. Two notarial acts were drawn up, couched in very similar terms, recording the names of those present at the assemblies and the religious houses that they represented, and providing a formal statement of their consent to the royal subsidy. It is noteworthy that at both meetings laymen as well as clerks were present: leading officials of the seneschalcies of Carcassonne and Toulouse were at Béziers and several knights, including Guillaume Aycellin, acting in lieu of the *bailli* of Auvergne, were at Clermont-Ferrand. In these circumstances evidence of opposition to the king's demands from the exempt abbeys and priories is hardly to be expected, and especially since both these assemblies followed shortly after provincial councils in which assent had been given to the grants. In both cases the notarial record of the consent to the subsidy is no more than a formal statement, which declares that the grants were made under the same terms and conditions already accepted by the non-exempt clergy.

The assembly at Béziers was not as large as the later one at Clermont-Ferrand. At Béziers twenty-six abbots, priors and proctors were in attendance, representing a total of thirty-three houses in the province of Narbonne; but, if small, it was an assembly of weight, for a large number of abbots attended in person: the abbots of Alet, St-Pons-de-Thomières, Fontcaude, Lagrasse, Joncels, St-Thibéry, St-Guilhem-le-Désert, St-Gilles and Psalmody. At Clermont-Ferrand three abbots attended in person (La Chaise-Dieu, Aurillac and Gaillac) and seventeen priors, along with eighteen proctors, all of these representing a total of sixty-two named exempt houses in the province of Bourges (dependencies were not always named). Many of the priories were dependent upon abbeys situated outside the particular province, and this was especially true in the case of the province of Bourges: among the external abbeys with dependent priories were, notably, St-Denis-en-France, Fleury, Fontevrault, St-Michel de Cluse, Vézelay, and St-Victor Marseilles. With very few exceptions the houses represented in both assemblies were Benedictine: Bonnevaux was a house of regular canons of the order of St-Ruf,[56] Brioude was a secular college and Port-Sainte-Marie was Carthusian. One house, La Capelette, was Premonstratensian; but the Premonstratensian abbots were, as we shall see, to hold a separate assembly

---

[55] For Pierre see Elizabeth A.R.BROWN, Royal commissioners and grants of privilege in Philip the Fair's France..., in Francia, 13, 1985, p. 153.

[56] For the order of St-Ruf see Jacques HOURLIER, L'âge classique 1140-1378: les religieux (Histoire du droit et des institutions de l'église en occident, ed. Gabriel LE BRAS, 10), pp. 90-1.

for their order. Although several monasteries from the exempt diocese of Le Puy were certainly represented at Clermont-Ferrand, including the abbey of St-Chaffre, it does not appear that either the bishop of Le Puy or the cathedral chapter in fact attended the assembly. Perhaps the bishop and cathedral church were more reluctant than the Benedictines to respond to a direct summons to a royal assembly; it would be rash, however, to assume from their absence that they did not contribute to the tax.

In addition to the provincial assemblies of non-exempt and of exempt clergy, separate meetings were held by the three major exempt orders of Cluny, Cîteaux and Prémontré. The Cluniac assembly held at Sens before 3 October 1294 was both the earliest and the largest, for all the abbots and priors of the order in France had been summoned to it.(C1) The preamble to the grant by the Cluniac order is stridently royalist in tone. The abbots of the Premonstratensian order met early in February 1295 at St-Quentin in the diocese of Noyon and the abbot of Prémontré's letter granting a subsidy (I) follows *mutatis mutandis* the preamble and terms of the grant from the provincial council of Rheims held four months earlier. The undated grant from the Cistercian order (K2), which resulted from a meeting of the Cistercian abbots of Cîteaux, La Ferté, Pontigny, Clairvaux and Morimond at Dijon, though distinct in some of its wording, also follows the pattern of other grants (compare the beginning of the preamble and clauses (v) (vi) and (vii) with E1, I1, and J1). There was some debate within the Cistercian order about the taxation of income from lands which were not within the kingdom of France (K1) and there was probably, too, some delay in the making of the grant, or in implementing the decision, for a letter from the king of June 1295 (K4) implies that the seneschal of Beaucaire or his agents had seized Cistercian goods because of non-payment. Even so, it needs to be stressed that the evidence for resistance from the Cistercians to royal taxation seems to post-date the demands of 1294-5. As Kervyn de Lettenhove revealed, it is certainly true that the register of the abbey of Dunes contains impressive evidence of the determination of the Cistercians to defend traditional clerical rights in the face of the king's policies,[57] but their opposition is not evident at this stage and seems to emerge during the first clash between the king and Boniface VIII, concerning taxation, in 1296-7. And what Kervyn de Lettenhove interpreted as an appeal to the pope as early as 1292 against the usurpations of Philip was in fact simply a declaration by the abbots of Cîteaux and Clairvaux that they were doing all in their power to obey papal orders concerning a papal tenth.[58] In 1294-5 the Cistercian order submitted to the king's demands in the same way as did the rest of the French clergy.

---

[57]KERVYN DE LETTENHOVE, Etudes (see n. 29), cols. 1840-5.

[58]See above n. 29.

Throughout the realm the biennial tenth was granted only on certain conditions. One of the conditions was that the clergy should themselves retain control over its collection. Time and again the grants make this clear. The pattern of the papal tenths was being consciously followed. In the provincial councils each bishop was responsible for the collection in his own diocese; in the provinces of Rheims and Lyons the two diocesan collectors were specified as a canon of the cathedral church and a nominee of the bishop, and we know that in the diocese of Bourges the collectors were a canon of Bourges and the chancellor of Bourges (A4b). The exempt of Bourges named the prior of Chirac as collector, who could choose deputies to act for him in each diocese. The abbots of St Martin Laon and Cuissy were named by the Premonstratensians, while the money was to be collected in each 'chamber' (*cameraria*) of the Cluniac order and for each 'family' (*generatio*) of the Cistercian order. Having been collected by the clergy themselves, the money was then to be paid to the king's deputies in accordance with royal instructions.

The agreed dates for the collection of the tax were often similar, though in none of the known cases identical. There were two terms for each year, around the spring of 1295 (at various dates between February and June) and the autumn of 1295, and the same terms in 1296. But the terms for the diocese of Rheims were unusually early (the first being 25 December 1294 and the last 24 June 1296); and for the diocese of Lyons they were unusually late, in fact a whole year later than for Rheims. The fact that this biennial tenth continued to be collected over so long a period is important to bear in mind. It had certainly not been fully collected by the time that Boniface VIII's famous prohibition of clerical taxation without papal licence, 'Clericis laicos', was issued (dated 24/25 February 1296 but not published in France until the summer).[59] Indeed, the first crisis between king and pope that resulted from this bull was almost over by the time that the final payment from the diocese of Lyons had become due. Also, other taxation demands had already intervened. Even though it is clear that the terms for the diocese of Lyons were exceptionally late, it seems likely, then, that many of the last payments to the king from the biennial tenth, including probably arrears, were curtailed by the pope's intervention.

Some understanding of the process of collection by the royal agents in 1295 and 1296 can be gained from Mignon's list of accounts and from a surviving account dated 1 November 1296 of receipts at the treasury of the Louvre.[60] But this evidence of accounts and receipts is so incomplete that

---

[59]DENTON (see n. 7), pp. 89-94.

[60]Inventaire, ed. LANGLOIS (see n. 18), nos. 701-11, 752 and Comptes du Trésor 1296, 1316, 1384, 1477, ed. Robert FAWTIER (Recueil des historiens de France, Documents financiers II, Paris, 1930), nos. 74, 93, 275-7, 279-80, 403.

no firm conclusions are possible about the rate or the success of the collection of the biennial tenth. It is nonetheless certain that money flowed in from a number of dioceses, sometimes named, in the provinces of Bordeaux, Sens, Rouen, Bourges, Narbonne, Lyons, Tours, Rheims and Auch, and also from the Cluniac order. Biche and Mouche Guidi, the king's well-known financial advisers, who were acting as treasurers of France in 1295,[61] played an active part in the collection. They had already received money from the diocese of Bourges by February 1295,(A4b) and some of the collectors named as presenting accounts were their proctors. As an indication that collection may well have been interrupted by 'Clericis laicos', none of the accounts listed by Mignon refers clearly to the collection of any instalment due later than the summer of 1296. This is not to suggest, of course, that some accounts were not presented after this time. Indeed, one of the accounts was presented as late as 25 September 1310: it was then that Pierre de Senochiis rendered his account for the biennial tenth from the diocese of Chartres for the two terms of the first year and the first term of the second year.

Even if the tax was not collected *in toto* it certainly provided the king with much-needed resources at a time of a crisis. At a low estimate 250,000 *livres tournois* may have been collected for the first year[62] and 125,000 *livres tournois* for the second year (on the assumption that the second term may not have been paid). The possible total of 375,000 *livres tournois* was the equivalent of about 107,000 pounds sterling,[63] corresponding closely to the amount demanded from the English clergy, for a half of their assessed income was £105,000. The English clergy, however, were required to contribute this much greater percentage of their income within eight months, and three-quarters of it had been paid by September 1295.[64] Clearly the French clergy were not being put under anything like the same degree of financial pressure as the English clergy. In addition, the concessions which Philip made to his clergy in respect of the biennial tenths were of much greater substance than the grudging responses of Edward to the English clergy's petitions.[65] The basic concessions of the French crown were in all probability made, at the king's or his advisers' initiative, in advance of the ecclesiastical assemblies, for the sets of conditions which the clergy attached

---

[61]STRAYER, Philip the Fair (see n. 9), p. 50.

[62]See above p. 10 and n. 33.

[63]On the basis of 3.5 to 1: see Peter SPUFFORD, Handbook of medieval exchange, Royal Historical Society, London, 1986, pp. 174, 198. PRESTWICH (see n. 7), p. 387n suggests about 4 to 1 for 1294.

[64]DENTON (see n. 7), p. 76.

[65]POWICKE and CHENEY (see n. 2), pp. 1132-3.

to their grants were very similar to each other, and quite often the items are identical.

These important conditions are easily summarised. The proviso that the clergy themselves were to be responsible for the collection of the tax has already been discussed.[66] Also, non-payment was to be dealt with by ecclesiastical censure without secular interference.[67] The clergy should be asked to pay no other royal or baronial subsidy.[68] The collection of the tax would cease if there was peace or a truce,[69] and would cease, too, if the papacy demanded a tenth.[70] The granting of the tax should not be prejudicial to the clergy in the future,[71] and royal letters patent should be issued stating that the subsidy had been conceded out of pure grace ('ex sola gratia et mera liberalitate').[72] In some sets of conditions there is an occasional additional item of local or particular significance, but in total these supplementary items are very few. It might well be imagined that behind these sets of conditions there lies a royal document to which the clergy were giving assent, and that in editing all these texts it would have been instructive to attempt to re-construct this document by textual analysis. It seems certain that the king and his agents were, indeed, giving the lead to the clergy in the making of conditions, but, with the exception of the grants made by the council of Rheims and the assembly of Premonstratensian abbots, which are virtually identical (E1 and I1), the terms of the clerical grants are in fact quite varied and distinct, so that there could well have been more than one documentary prototype for the letters of acceptance of the tax. And, in any case, as was indicated in respect of the papally-ordered councils of 1292,[73] it is more than likely that there was communication between councils and assemblies, even when they were held in different parts of the realm, and that the groups of clergy thus influenced each other in the decisions that were taken and in the terms of their letters to the king.

It is hard to imagine in the circumstances of 1294 any additional provisos, concerning their rights in relation to taxation, that could have been

---

[66]Above p. 21.

[67]D2 viii, E1 iii and I1 iii.

[68]A3 vii & viii, C1 viii, D2 vi, J1 vii and L1 v & vi.

[69]A3 iii, C1 vi, D2 iv & v, E1 vi & vii, I1 vi & vii, J1 iii & iv, K2 vi & vii and L1 iii & iv. And see Elizabeth A.R.BROWN, *Cessante causa* and the taxes of the last Capetians: the political application of a philosophical maxim, in Studia Gratiana, 15, 1972, pp. 567-87.

[70]C1 v, D2 iii, E1 v, I1 v, J1 v, K2 v and L1 ii.

[71]A3 x, C1 vii, D2 ii, J1 ix and K2 viii.

[72]A3 ix, D2 x and J1 viii; and for the royal letters see see A4a, C2I and L1.

[73]Above p. 8.

granted to the clergy. Philip the Fair had made every effort to ensure acceptance of his request for a subsidy. He may have acted summarily in issuing a direct citation to the bishop of Uzès and there was clearly no precedent for the holding of royal assemblies of exempt clergy,[74] but the principle of clerical consent to taxation was being fully respected. In one unusual clause in the grant from the clergy of the province of Bourges (A3 ii) reference was made to the need for a papal licence: 'saving the goodwill in these matters of our lord the pope'. But it was immediately added that perhaps the emergency was so great that it was not possible to await the permission of the pope without danger to the realm. This clause can hardly be understood strictly speaking as a condition, since the clergy of Bourges were quite clearly making a grant without any anticipation that the pope would in fact be approached. Even so, the clause was surely not included simply because they wished to pay lip service to the canonical principle of papal consent. They recognised that they were in something of a dilemma. It was as much the duty of the clergy as of the king to seek papal permission, but they seem to have been trying to get out of their dilemma by putting onto the king's shoulders the responsibility of judging the degree of necessity and of seeking papal permission if possible. The nature of the emergency must certainly have been a crucial issue in the discussion at Bourges and elsewhere, and the king and his agents certainly persuaded the clergy that the imminent danger to the realm necessitated immediate financial assistance, even though canon law required papal agreement.[75] While Nicholas IV had failed to convince them that the defence of the Holy Land was a matter of *urgens necessitas*, two and a half years later Philip IV won his argument concerning the defence of the realm against the English and, in effect, took over the papal taxes.

How far the French clergy were pressured into acting against their better judgment is difficult to estimate. But there is no doubting the skill with which royal policy was executed and no doubting, too, the clergy's general, if in some instances rather tardy, acquiescence. The king's success is surely demonstrated by the fact that even the clergy of the province of Bordeaux granted the biennial tenth. On the analogy of the noble support in Gascony for Edward I,[76] it might well have been supposed that Philip would have had difficulty in gaining clerical backing from the region of Aquitaine; but

---

[74]Above pp. 7, 18-20.

[75]The suggestion that the Tours clergy gained the consent of the pope is based upon a misreading of the text: Les conciles de Tours, ed. AVRIL (see n. 1), pp. 307, 311 n. 2.

[76]Malcolm G.A.VALE, The Gascon nobility and the Anglo-French war 1294-98, in War and government in the middle ages: essays in honour of J.O.Prestwich, ed. John GILLINGHAM and J.C.HOLT (Bury St Edmunds, 1984), pp. 134-46.

collection of the taxes was certainly undertaken, at least in the dioceses of Bordeaux, Périgueux and Agen.

The best-known sections of the letters conceding subsidies are the preambles which justify the king's need and praise the French monarchy. As with the lists of conditions, we might well suspect that here too we can hear the voice of the king and his advisers rather than that of the clergy. This may well be true in the case of the identical wording of the letter from the clergy of the Rheims province (E1) and the letter from the Premonstratensian abbots (I1), abbreviated a little in the letter from the Lyons province (J1) and greatly abbreviated in the letter from the Cistercian abbots (K2). This justificatory prologue with its initial reference to knowledge of the 'blessed kingdom of France' being conveyed to the whole world 'from olden times' is reminiscent of the royalist tract, of only two years or so later, which begins 'Before there were clerks'.[77] The clergy were making their grants to the king in terms which stressed that as of old the French kingdom, surpassing all other kingdoms, provided defence for the orthodox faith and invincible protection for catholic purity. Within this kingdom peace had always flourished, the catholic faith prospered and the Christian religion enjoyed fruitful growth. Under Philip and his progenitors the Gallican Church had been endowed with the sweetness and repose of peace and, God willing, the clergy would enjoy forever that mutual charity in which churchmen, princes and magnates lived together. This eulogy of king and kingdom, emphatically within the context of devotion to the French clergy and the French church, is followed by an attack upon the villainy and machinations of the king of England. The actions of their own king had the support of God (*auctore domino*), whereas the king of England, famed for his notorious excesses and his manifest crimes, acted at the urging of the Devil (*suadente diabolo*). Can there be any doubt that the war against Edward I had been turned into a holy war? But, however much French interests via Charles of Naples influenced Celestine V in his brief period of office (5 July to 13 December 1294), it was a holy war without any kind of papal backing.

If the clerical grants had been made only within the set terms of the letters from Rheims and Lyons, and from the Premonstratensian and Cistercian abbots, it would have been easy to imagine that the arguments were little more than royal propaganda, that is beliefs to which the clergy only formally, even perhaps reluctantly, adhered. But the clergy of the province of Tours and the Cluniac abbots prefaced their grants with apparently quite independent statements which were even more stridently royalist in tone. The Tours clergy (D2) raised their grant to the level of an act of natural reason, supporting as it did the wondrous and praiseworthy

---

[77] Antequam essent clerici: Pierre DUPUY, Histoire du différend d'entre le pape Boniface VIII et Philippe le Bel roy de France, Paris, 1655, pp. 21-3.

devotion of the blessed kingdom of France and the ineffable munificence of their kings towards churches. The terms become ever more lavish: the kingdom provided the very foundation of holy religion, was the pillar and the shield of the church, the protector of the faith, the source of wisdom irrigating the whole world. For this reason God raised their kingdom above all other kingdoms and granted them victory and triumph over their enemies. And the ensuing attack upon Edward I could hardly have been more vicious: 'spewing out his venom from viscera poisoned long before'. The Cluniac abbots wrote in similarly startling phrases (C1), eloquently stressing the fervent devotion to Christ of Philip the Fair and his predecessors, with the result that any danger to the king and the kingdom must be seen as a danger to the universal Church. The king's cause was God's cause, and aid to the king was essential for the preservation of peace and the welfare of the Church.

In the autumn of 1294 the French Crown had created among some influential sectors of French society what can only be described as war fever. The arguments put forward by a significant slice, at least, of both the secular and the regular clergy must, it seems, be accepted as representing a strong, current ecclesiastical viewpoint. But fever rarely lasts. The clergy knew that they were acting in an emergency. They were making an exceptional grant in exceptional circumstances. The arguments of immediate need and imminent danger would be difficult to maintain, and Philip had set himself the difficult task of holding on to the full allegiance, and the continuing financial backing, of his clergy. Behind the strong words of support for the king there was the real world of clashes with royal officials and doubts about royal policies. This is illustrated clearly in respect of the clergy of the province of Tours. Their letter to Philip praised the most Christian kings of the French who, more than all other kings, had founded monasteries, given splendid endowments to churches, honouring them with privileges of immunity and liberty; but a contemporary set of grievances from the bishop of Angers, which could possibly be associated with the very council at which their grant was made, adds that in modern times the churches and monasteries founded by the most sacred princes are being destroyed, exhausted and confounded, and the former devotion of the most sacred princes has ceased and has given way to the oppression of churches.[78] The complaints to the king reveal a different clerical viewpoint. Certainly we must not assume that clerical support for the king in 1294 and 1295 was unthinking and uncritical. Nor must we assume that the failure to seek papal consent implied a lack of contact with the papal curia, for in September 1294 seven French prelates

---

[78]Livre, ed. PORT (see n. 25), p. 329 and Les conciles de Tours, ed. AVRIL (see n. 1), pp. 308-10. For another set of grievances in 1294, from the bishop of Uzès, see Léon MENARD, Histoire civile ecclésiastique et littéraire de la ville de Nisme, 1750, 1, preuves pp. 118-22.

had become cardinals, among them Simon of Beaulieu, archbishop of Bourges, Berald of Got, archbishop of Lyons, and the canonist John the Monk, bishop-elect of Arras.[79] Nevertheless the actions of the French clergy had profound implications for their future relations with both the Crown and the papacy. When Boniface VIII was elected pope on Christmas Eve 1294, they were in the process of giving full support, from their spiritual and temporal income, to a war, as it was claimed, in defence of the faith. But could they do so without the support of the pope? Anglo-French bitterness and the dilemma of the French clergy were not of Boniface VIII's making; but they were problems which he could not for long ignore.

[79]The rest were William of Ferrières, provost of Marseilles, Nicholas of Nonancour, dean of Notre-Dame Paris, Robert abbot of Cîteaux and Simon prior of the Cluniac house of La Charité. See Peter HERDE, Cölestin V 1294, Stuttgart, 1981, pp. 100-4.

CONTENTS OF APPENDICES

APPENDICES

In the following texts place-names have been identified with the assistance of the Dictionnaire nationale des communes de France (1984). Round brackets have been used for editorial comments and square brackets for additions to the text by way of suggested emendation. Variant spellings in the texts have been for the most part retained, but punctuation and capitalisation are the editor's, i is used for i and j, u is used for the vowel and v for the consonant, and, in accordance with classical practice, t is used where some manuscripts have c. Abbreviations: AD = Archives Départementales; AM = Archives Municipales; AN = Archives Nationales; and BN = Bibliothèque Nationale.

Appendix A. COUNCIL OF THE PROVINCE OF BOURGES AT AURILLAC, 26-29 SEPTEMBER 1294

On 31 July the archbishop of Bourges, Simon de Beaulieu, ordered his suffragan bishop of Clermont to summon all the non-exempt bishops and clergy of the province of Bourges to attend a council at Aurillac on 26 September. The surviving writ from the bishop of Clermont (1) is addressed to the bishop of Albi, and writs in the same form were no doubt also sent to the other four bishoprics of the province (not including, naturally, the bishopric of Le Puy which was exempt from the archbishop's authority), that is the bishoprics of Limoges, Cahors, Rodez and Mende. The higher clergy were to attend in person and the lower clergy by proctors. All the bishops attended, with the exception only of Limoges, the see of which was vacant at the time.[80] The archbishop, however, had been summoned to Rome and was made cardinal and bishop of Palestrina on 18 September,[81] and the council was thus presided over by the archbishop's official, master Jean de Gessia (see 2 & 3). The *terminus ad quem* for the council is provided by the date of the grant of a subsidy (3). It is interesting that the famous canonist, William Durand, bishop of Mende, was present at these proceedings, for his Speculum Iuris, as we would expect, contains a statement of the immunity of churches and churchmen from exactions by anyone exercising secular jurisdiction.[82]

1 Summons to the Council

Once in the archive of the bishop of Albi and printed here from the late seventeenth-century copy in BN Baluze 6, fos. 6r-7v. Also copied accurately in 1669 from the same source in BN Doat 11, fos. 161v-164v. The archbishop's mandate is printed in MARTENE & DURAND (see n. 5), 4, pp. 213-14.

Reverendo in Christo patri domino dei gratia episcopo Albiensi Ademarus permissione eiusdem Claromontensis episcopus salutem et sinceram in domino caritatem. Noveritis nos litteras domini Bituricensis archiepiscopi Aquitanie primatis recepisse in hec verba: Simon dei gratia Bituricensis archiepiscopus Aquitanie primas venerabili fratri A. eiusdem gratia

---

[80]Conrad EUBEL, Hierarchia catholica medii aevi (1198-1431), Regensberg, 1898, 1, p. 313.

[81]Ibid, p. 11 and HERDE (see n. 79). And see John MARRONE & Charles ZUCKERMAN, 'Cardinal Simon de Beaulieu and relations between Philip the Fair and Boniface VIII', in Traditio, 31, 1975, pp. 195-222.

[82]William DURAND, Speculum iuris, Basle, 1574, 2, p. 437 (Lib. 3 pt 3, de immunitate ecclesiarum), and see DIGARD (see n. 17), 1, p. 259.

Claromontensi episcopo salutem et sinceram in domino caritatem. In firmamento celi scilicet universalis ecclesie a deo facta fuerunt duo luminaria, id est institute due dignitates, videlicet pontificalis auctoritas et regalis potestas, a quarum qualibet gubernari et regi debent subditi ut sub omni quiete consistant, quod in regno Francie per compassiones et supportationes mutuas actore domino est hactenus observatum. Nos itaque qui pontificali licet indigni fungimur dignitate in dicto regno in parte sollicitudinis evocati merito formidamus ne sanguis subditorum nostrorum de nostris manibus requiratur, nisi contra turbatores quietis publice ascendamus ex adverso et nos murum opponamus pro defensione fidei et reipublice clericorum et ad perfecte observantiam caritatis, ac ob hoc principaliter pretextu cuiusdam tractatus habiti cum excellentissimo principe ac domino domino Philippo dei gratia rege Francorum una cum archiepiscopis regni eiusdem super imminentibus et arduis negotiis, que totum regnum ipsum et quascumque personas eiusdem regni ad cuius turbationem aspirat hostilis seditio dinoscuntur tangere, dispendioso quarum periculo ut quieta sibi tranquillitas preparetur dignum et pium est auctoritatis pontificalis potentieque regalis clipeis obviare, nec non super quibusdam aliis statum ecclesiarum et personarum ecclesiasticarum nostre provincie [tangentibus] que celeritatem desiderant tractandis et feliciter promovendis, una cum suffraganeis nostris capitulis decanis archidiaconis abbatibus conventualibus et collegiatarum ecclesiarum prioribus archipresbyteris ecclesiarum rectoribus perpetuis vicariis et aliis clericis beneficiatis provincie nostre Bituricensis in quacumque dignitate officio vel ordine constitutis, quos universos et singulos negotium presens tangit et propter [hoc] ab omnibus approbandum, tractare salubriter disposuimus in instanti concilio quod die dominica post festum sancti Mathei apostoli proxime venturum (*26 September*) et diebus sequentibus si quos continuari contigerit seu etiam prorogari apud Aureliacum Claromontensis diocesis, ob universalis ecclesie totius provincie Bituricensis et reipublice utilitatem ac necessitatem urgentem immo potius imminentem,[83] ad instar aliorum archiepiscoporum eiusdem regni, vestris parcentes laboribus et expensis sicut vobis hiis temporibus oretenus exponemus, domino concedente proponimus celebrare. Fraternitati vestre mandamus quatenus omnes et singulos suffraganeos nostros capitula ecclesiarum cathedralium et collegiatarum decanos archidiaconos et alios in ecclesiis collegiatis secularibus dignitatem seu personatum habentes abbates conventuales et collegiatarum vel non collegiatarum ecclesiarum priores archipresbyteros et decanos rurales ecclesiarum rectores et alias personas predictas in dicta Bituricensi provincia constitutas citetis peremptorie et vocetis seu citari et vocari peremptorie faciatis, ut ipsi dictis diebus et loco ad dictum concilium, videlicet episcopi

---

[83]eminentem MS *and* Doat 11, fo. 163r.

decani archidiaconi abbates conventuales et ecclesiarum collegiatarum priores et alie persone dignitatem habentes pro se personaliter, capitula collegia archipresbyteri decani rurales ecclesiarum rectores et alie inferioris ordinis sive persone status per procuratores sive yconomos sufficienter instructos, compareant audituri tractaturi obligaturi si necesse fuerit facturi et adimpleturi quidquid in dicto concilio audiendum faciendum tractandum ordinandum et per obligationem adimplendum fuerit super premissis et ea tangentibus, ad que peremptorie vos citamus similiter et vocamus, vobis mandantes ut subditos vestros citari et vocari faciatis secundum formam superius annotatam. Volumus si quidem ac etiam indulgemus quod per vos et alios suffraganeos vestros videlicet per quemlibet in sua civitate et diocesi cum eorum suffraganeorum subditis quos citari personaliter mandavimus dispensare possitis ex causa legitima, ut dictis diebus et loco comparare valeant per procuratorem sufficienter instructum prout superius est expressum, causam dispensationis vestris conscientiis relinquentes. Incessus autem vestros vos et alii sic maturare curetis, quod dicta die dominica de premissis negotiis ad expeditionem subditorum celerem aliquid inchoare possimus. Datum apud Sanctum Audoenum die sabbati post octavas festi beate Marie Magdalene anno domini millesimo ducentesimo nonagesimo quarto septima indictione. (*St-Ouen, 31 July 1294*) Iuxta quarum continentiam et mandatum auctoritate predicta vobis iniungimus et mandamus quatinus omnes et singulos et subditos vestros prout in dictis litteris continetur citetis vel citari et vocari faciatis ad prefatum concilium in locum predictum, et predicta omnia et singula faciatis prout in mandato prescripto dicti domini archiepiscopi videbitis contineri. Nos enim vos tenore presentium ad premissa peremptorie citamus similiter et vocamus, certificantes nos per vestras patentes litteras nobis per latorem presentium dirigendas de citatione visione receptione presentium litterarum, ut vos et nos non possimus de negligentia seu contemptu in aliquo reprehendi. Datum die lune post festum assumptionis beate Marie gloriose anno domini millesimo ducentesimo nonagesimo quarto. (*16 August 1294*)

2 **Statement by the archbishop's official concerning the terms of the summons**
Once in the archive of the bishop of Albi and printed here from the copy in BN Baluze 6, fos. 5r-v & 15r. Also copied in BN Doat 11, fos. 174r-175v; and printed in MARTENE & DURAND (see n. 5), 4, pp. 214-15.

Nos officialis Bituricensis gerens vices reverendi in Christo patris domini S. dei gratia Bituricensis archiepiscopi Aquitanieque primatis in congregatione apud Aureliacum Claromontensis diocesis habita ob necessitatem regni Francie et ad requisitionem domini regis Francie, data dominica post festum beati Mathei apostoli ac diebus sequentibus continuatis, notum facimus universis quod cum idem dominus archiepiscopus mandaverit evocari subditos suffraganeorum suorum ad dictam congregationem, scilicet decanos prepositos et abbates seculares archidiaconos archipresbyteros priores simplices non collegiatos decanos rurales capellanos rectores ecclesiarum et perpetuos vicarios abbates et priores religiosos ceterosque clericos beneficiatos cuiuscumque ordinis sive status sub forma que sequitur: Simon etc, dictique decani prepositi et abbates seculares archipresbyteri priores simplices non collegiati decani rurales capellani rectores ecclesiarum perpetuique vicarii abbates et priores religiosi et conventus ceterique clerici beneficiati cuiuscumque ordinis sive status vel procuratores[84] ipsorum conquererentur et dicerent predictum mandatum factum in eorum preiudicium et gravamen et contra antiquam observantiam et canonicas sanctiones, cum idem dominus archiepiscopus in ipsos nullam potestatem vel iurisdictionem habeat in hoc casu, et peterent ac requirerent instanter mandatum huiusmodi quatenus contra eos de facto processerat revocari et penitus anullari, nos habito et obtento consilio ac consensu reverendorum patrum A. Claromontensis et S. Caturcensis R. Ruthenensis B. Albiensis Guillelmi Mimatensis dei gratia episcoporum in ipsa convocatione presentium, volentes predictis conquerentibus esse prompti et benivoli in iustitia facienda nolumus nec intendimus quod per mandatum huiusmodi factum dictis conquerentibus vel aliis quibuscumque aliquod preiudicium generetur, nec alicui sententie vel processui eos subiacere volumus contra non venientes ad concilium promulgate in quantum eis ex hoc novum preiudicium pararetur, volentes insuper et expressum dantes assensum una cum predictis dominis episcopis quod ex dicto mandato vel aliquo ex eo vel ob id facto aliquod ius in proprietate possessione vel quasi acrescat vel decrescat de novo eidem domino archiepiscopo vel ecclesie sue Bituricensi seu etiam acquiratur. Datum et actum apud Aureliacum tertio kalendas Octobris anno domini millesimo ducentesimo nonagesimo quarto. (*29 September 1294*)

3   Grant of biennial tenth

Printed here from original in AN J1035 no. 38: 24cm. X 28cm. + 3cm. (pli); six seal tags and remnants of three seals; on dorse in contemporary hand 'littera decime provincie Bituricensis'. Also, an original and a copy were once in the archive of the bishop of Albi, whence BN Baluze 6, fos. 8r-9v, 10r-11v, BN Doat 11, fos. 166r-169v, 170r-173v, and MARTENE & DURAND (see n. 5), 4, pp. 215-17.

Notum sit omnibus presentis scripture seriem inspecturis quod nos miseratione divina infrascripti episcopi et magister Johannes de Gessia officialis Bituricensis et gerens vices reverendi patris domini S. dei gratia Bituricensis archiepiscopi Aquitanieque primatis in remotis agentis nec non et capitulorum kathedralium et aliarum collegiatarum ecclesiarum procuratores decani abbates quoque et priores conventuales non exempti et

---

[84]procurator MS.

totum consilium provincie Bituricensis ad vocationem reverendi patris domini archiepiscopi supradicti apud Aureliacum Claromontensis dyocesis ad tactandum ibidem super necessitatibus et utilitatibus ecclesiarum et ecclesiasticarum personarum ipsius provincie et insuper super pacifico et tranquillo statu totius regni Francie constituti, sedula[85] meditatione pensantes quod nonnulli principes et magnates regnum ipsum invadere et a diversis eius lateribus illud hostiliter inpugnare dei timore postposito moliuntur, idcirco dignum ducimus eidem domino regi in tante necessitatis articulo assistere eique prout ad presens est possibile subvenire. Diligenti igitur tractatu et deliberatione prehabitis, unanimiter concedimus et promittimus eidem domino regi dare pro tuitione et deffensione regni sui decimam omnium proventuum ecclesiasticorum totius Bituricensis provincie per duos annos ab hac die continue computandos, sub[86] modo tamen et temperamentis ac conditionibus infrascriptis. (i) Volumus enim et ordinamus quod terminus prime solutionis primi anni faciende sit in instanti Carniprivio (*20 February, i.e. beginning of Lent 1295*), terminus vero secunde solutionis primi anni sit in festo Omnium Sanctorum (*1 November*) extunc proxime subsequenti, solutiones vero anni secundi fiant anno revoluto eisdem temporibus. (ii) Hoc autem facimus et concedimus salvo in his domini nostri summi pontificis beneplacito voluntatis, nisi forte tanta et tam evidens regni eiusdem immineret necessitas, quod absque grandi ipsius periculo non posset voluntas ipsius domini summi pontificis expectari. (iii) Sed et si infra memoratos faciendarum solutionum terminos pacem vel treugam fieri contigerit, vel alias regni ipsius periculum cessaverit, concessio et promissio huiusmodi pro tempore tunc futuro omnino cessent et pro infectis habeantur vel propter treugam quantum treuga duraverit prolongentur. (iv) Ad hec si interim onus simile vel equipollens in quotitate vel quantitate quacumque per alium quemcumque inponi ecclesie Gallicane vel iam inpositum exigi contingeret, cui inpositioni vel exactioni prelati cum iustitia resistere nequirent, hoc quidem casu dictum subsidium volumus similiter omnino cessare. (v) Volumus insuper et ordinamus quod decima seu subsidium huiusmodi levetur per dominum Bituricensem et per episcopos eius suffraganeos in suis dyocesibus seu per substitutos ab eis de beneficiis et a personis solvere decimam solitis, iuxta ordinationes et declarationes Romanorum pontificum et legatorum apostolice sedis olim editas super solutione decime aliis ex causis preteritis temporibus persolute, nisi forte in iuris subsidium manus regia per eosdem specialiter fuerit requisita, quodque ipsi potestatem habeant videlicet quilibet in sua civitate et dyocesi quoslibet ad solutionem dicte decime seu subsidii per censuram ecclesiasticam

---

[85]cedula MS.

[86]sub *interlined*

compellendi et excommunicatos interdictos propter hoc vel suspensos a sententiis huiusmodi absolvendi. (vi) Volumus etiam ad tollenda multa incommoda atque dampna quod huius decime seu subsidii solutio fiat de peccunia communiter currente in loco de quo peccuniam ipsam levari continget. (vii) Rursus intelligimus et hoc a regia maiestate humiliter postulamus quod nullus prelatus nullaque ecclesiastica persona in hoc subsidio contribuens ad cavalcatas seu alia armorum subsidia vel ad alia etiam hac[87] occasione honera insolita et indebita interim compellatur aut super his molestetur. (viii) Quodque idem dominus rex non sinat aliud exigi subsidium ab ecclesiis seu ecclesiasticis personis aut aliud honus insolitum eis inponi occasione huiusmodi guerre per comites vicecomites barones vel alias quascumque seculares personas in terris eorum. (ix) Quodque ipse dominus rex debeat concedere suas patentes litteras reverendo patri domino Bituricensi archiepiscopo[88] et omnibus subfraganeis suis pro se et eorum subditis continentes quod ipse subsidium huiusmodi ex sola gratia et mera liberalitate recipit. (x) Quodque per hoc nullum inposterum ecclesiis et personis ecclesiasticis memorate provincie preiudicium quomodolibet generetur. In quorum omnium testimonium nos A. Claromontensis S. Caturcensis R. Ruthenensis B. Albyensis et G. Mimatensis miseratione divina episcopi et magister Johannes de Gessia officialis Bituricensis sigillorum nostrorum inpressiones huic scripture duximus appendendas. Datum et actum apud Aureliacum iii[o] kalendas Octobris anno domini millesimo ducentesimo nonagesimo quarto. (*29 September 1294*)

> **4   Royal acceptance of the tenth and the instructions of the collectors**
> Printed here from BN Baluze 6, fos. 12r-14v. Also in BN Doat 11, fos. 177r-183r. The king's letter of 10 Feb. is in MARTENE & DURAND (see n. 5), 4, pp. 217-18.

a) Philippus dei gratia Francorum rex universis presentes litteras inspecturis salutem. Notum facimus quod cum dilecti et fideles nostri archiepiscopus Bituricensis per officialem suum gerentemque ad hec vices ipsius archiepiscopi nunc in remotis agentis et omnes suffraganei Bituricensis ecclesie nec non et capitulorum cathedralium et aliarum ecclesiarum collegiatarum procuratores decani abbates priores conventuales non exempti et totum concilium provincie Bituricensis nuper ad vocationem predicti archiepiscopi apud Aureliacum Claromontensis diocesis constituti, ad pertractandum ibidem super pacifico et tranquillo statu totius regni nostri, sedula meditatione pensantes quod nonnulli principes et magnates regnum nostrum invadere et a diversis eius lateribus ibidem hostiliter impugnare dei timore postposito moliuntur, et idcirco ducentes nobis assistere in tante

---

[87]ac MS.

[88]episcopo MS.

necessitatis articulo et prout ad presens est possibile subvenire, diligenti tractatu et deliberatione prehabitis unanimiter et concorditer nobis dare promiserint et concesserint pro tuitione et deffensione regni nostri decimam omnium proventuum ecclesiasticorum totius Bituricensis provincie per duos annos a tempore concessionis huiusmodi computandos, sub quibusdam conditionibus et temperamentis adiectis appositis et contentis in litteris prelatorum predictorum quas vidimus confectis super concessione decime predicte, nos modos et conditiones contentos in dictis litteris huiusmodi confectis volumus concedimus ac etiam approbamus, et inhibemus districte omnibus subditis nostris ne contraveniant et ne contrarium quomodolibet attemptare presumant, et profitemur quod predicti prelati ex sola gratia et mera liberalitate predictum subsidium nobis faciunt et illud ab eisdem ex mera gratia recipimus, nec volumus quod per hec ipsis prelatis ecclesiis et ecclesiasticis personis ipsius provincie Bituricensis imposterum aliquod preiudicium generetur. In quorum testimonium presentibus litteris sigillum nostrum duximus apponendum. Actum Parisiis die iovis post octabas purificationis beate Marie virginis anno domini millesimo ducentesimo nonagesimo quarto. (*10 February 1295*)

b) Reverendo in Christo patri ac domino domino B. dei gratia Albiensi episcopo sui devoti magistri Egidius cancellarius Bituricensis et Johannes Gresillons Bituricensis canonicus, collectores decime illustri domino regi Francie concesse pro subsidio regni sui salutem et cum reverentia et honore paratam ad eius beneplacita voluntatem. Noveritis quod anno domini millesimo ducentesimo nonagesimo quinto die cinerum litteras predicti domini regis vidimus et recepimus in hec verba: Philippus .... (*as* a) *above*) Item et alias in hec verba: Philippus dei gratia Francorum rex dilecto et fideli nostro archiepiscopo Bituricensi salutem et dilectionem. Requirimus vos quatinus omnem pecuniam quam ex decima nobis a vobis et subditis vestris sub certa forma concessa in subsidium regni nostri hactenus levavistis et quam de cetero levabitis ex eadem receptoribus dilectis nostris Brichio et Moucheto Guidy vel eorum seu alterius eorundem procuratoribus tradatis et deliberetis sine delatione quacumque. De pecunia vero sibi vel eorum procuratoribus tradita tenore presentium vos quitamus. Actum Parisius die veneris ante cineres anno domini millesimo ducentesimo nonagesimo quarto. (*11 February 1295*) Hinc est quod significamus vobis quod nos procuratoribus predictorum Brichii et Moucheti tradidimus et deliberavimus quidquid receperamus de predicta pecunia primi termini et residuum quod adhuc recipiemus de dicto termino eisdem procuratoribus deliberabimus et trademus, et cum intelleximus et pro certo quod vos habetis litteras consimiles litteris predictis domini regis suprascriptis consulimus vobis salvo vestro meliori consilio quod illud quod recepistis et recipietis de dicta decima pro primo termino tradi et deliberari faciatis procuratoribus antedictis. Datum et sigillis nostris sigillatum anno et die cinerum predictis. (*16 February 1295*)

Appendix B.   ASSEMBLY OF THE EXEMPT CLERGY OF THE PROVINCE OF BOURGES AT CLERMONT-FERRAND, 8-9 NOVEMBER 1294
Summoned by the king for 8 November the assembly met in the chapter house of the Dominicans at Clermont-Ferrand and granted a subsidy on 9 November. See above pp. 18-20.

1   **Royal summons of the exempt of the province (a), writs concerning the names of those summoned (b, c) and a separate summons to the exempt diocese of Le Puy (d)**

Printed here from the copies in BN Lat. 11017 (a contemporary or near-contemporary register of the seneschalcy of Beaucaire), fos. 25r-26v (calendared in Eugène MARTIN-CHABOT, Les archives de la cour des comptes aides et finances de Montpellier: avec un essai de restitution des premiers registres de sénéchaussée (Bibliothèque de la Faculté des Lettres, 22, Paris, 1907), nos. 127-30). All but the first letter are also printed, from fos. 25v-26v, in MENARD (see n. 78), preuves, pp. 129-30.

a) Philippus dei gratia Francorum rex dilectis et fidelibus nostris abbatibus prioribus prepositis decanis capitulis conventibus collegiis ceterisque personis ecclesiasticis exemptis Bituricensis provincie ad quos presentes littere pervenerint salutem et dilectionem. Nuper in nostri tractatum extitit deliberatione consilii episcopos abbates prelatos priores prepositos decanos capitula conventus collegia tam cathedralium quam collegiatarum et conventualium rectoresque ecclesiarum et ceteras personas ecclesiasticas regni nostri exemptas et non exemptas, propter quedam ardua negotia generalem statum regni eiusdem ac ecclesiarum et ecclesiasticarum personarum tangentia que tractanda imminent hiis diebus, ad nostram presentiam convocare. Considerantes autem postmodum quod honerosum existeret et etiam sumptuosum singulos archiepiscopos episcopos abbates priores prepositos decanos capitula conventus collegia tam cathedralium quam collegiatarum et conventualium rectoresque ecclesiarum et ceteras personas ecclesiasticas regni nostri exemptas et etiam non exemptas in unum propter hoc convenire, ac volentes eis in hac parte consulere super laboribus et expensis, consilio deliberato providimus quod in unaquaque provincia abbates priores prepositi decani capitula conventus collegia alieque ecclesiastice persone eiusdem provincie exempte conveniant super huiusmodi negotiis tractaturi. Verum quia, sicut ex quorundam vestrum insinuatione accepimus, non consuevistis[89] hactenus certo loco in dicta provincia talia vel consimilia capitula celebrare, nec de huiusmodi loco possetis de facili convenire, universitatem vestram requirimus quatinus octava die instantis mensis Novembris apud Claromontem in Auvernia iuxta formam superius expressam interesse et comparere curetis. Actum Sanctum Germanium in Laya die iovis post festum sancti Bartholomei apostoli anno domini m⁰ cc⁰ lxxxx quarto. (*St-Germain-en-Laye, 26 August 1294*)

---

[89]consuevimus MS.

b) Philippus dei gratia Francorum rex dilectis et fidelibus suis collectoribus decime personarum ecclesiasticarum exemptarum provincie Bituricensis salutem et dilectionem. Cum ad presens sit necesse quod senescallus noster Bellicadri habeat nomina personarum ecclesiasticarum exemptarum civitatum et diocesium Mimatensis et Aniciensis, mandamus vobis quatinus indilate nomina personarum ecclesiaticarum exemptarum civitatum et diocesium predictarum transcribi faciatis et ea dicto senescallo nostro vel eius mandato tradatis, quando super hoc ab ipso senescallo vel eius mandato fueritis requisiti. Actum Parisius die lune post nativitatem beate Marie virginis anno domini millesimo ducentesimo nonagesimo quarto. (*13 September 1294*)

c) Philippus dei gratia Francorum rex senescallo Bellicadri salutem. Litteras nostras per presentium portitorem vobis mittimus personis ecclesiasticis exemptis civitatum et diocesium Mimatensis et Aniciensis super quibusdam negotiis regnum nostrum et ipsos tangentibus dirigendas, mandantes vobis quatinus recipiatis a collectoribus decime personarum ecclesiaticarum exemptarum provincie Bituricensis nomina personarum ecclesiasticarum exemptarum civitatum et diocesium Mimatensis et Aniciensis predictarum et mittatis dictis personis exemptis dictarum civitatum et diocesium per bonos et certos nuncios dictas litteras indilate. Tradidimus autem portitori presentium nostras litteras vobis tradendas dirigendas collectoribus decime personarum ecclesiasticarum exemptarum provincie Bituricensis, ut tradant vobis nomina personarum ecclesiastiarum dictarum civitatum et diocesium. Actum Parisius die lune post festum nativitatis beate Marie virginis anno domini millesimo ducentesimo nonagesimo quarto. (*13 September 1294*)

d) Philippus dei gratia Francorum rex dilectis et fidelibus nostris episcopo et capitulo Aniciensi abbatibus prioribus prepositis decanis capitulis conventibus collegiis ceterisque personis ecclesiasticis exemptis civitatis et dyocesis Aniciensis ad quos presentes littere pervenerint salutem et dilectionem. Nuper... (*as* a) *above, adding* episcopi *after* in unaquaque provincia *and deleting* in dicta provincia *after* hactenus certo loco) ...comparere curetis. Actum apud Parisius die veneris ante festum beati Michaelis anno domini millesimo ducentesimo nonagesimo quarto. (*24 September 1294*)

2   Grant of biennial tenth
Printed from AN J456 no. 31, 46 cm. X 60 cm., original notarial instrument with sign manual.

In nomine domini nostri Ihesu Christi amen. Anno incarnationis eiusdem m^o cc^o nonogesimo quarto, indictione octavo, pontificatus sanctissimi patris domini Celestini divina providentia pape quinti anno primo, mense Novembris octava die mensis eiusdem. (*8 November 1294*) Per hoc presens publicum instrumentum cunctis appareat evidenter quod, cum exempti Bituricensis provincie ad vocationem eis factam de mandato serenissimi principis domini Philippi dei gratia regis Francorum illustris citati essent apud Claromontem in Arvernia ad diem supradictam ad tractandum ordinandum concordandum et firmandum cum gentibus eiusdem domini regis super contentis in litteris regiis eisdem exemptis missis, ipsa inquam octava die comparuerunt apud Claromontem in presentia mei Johannis auctoritate sedis apostolice notarii publici et testium subscriptorum ad hoc specialiter vocatorum et rogatorum coram venerabilibus et discretis viris magistris G[erardo] de Malo Monte cantore Bituricense et P[etro] de Latilliaco canonico Suessionensis clericis dicti domini regis et pro presenti negotio per ipsum dominum regem ad Bituricensem provinciam destinatis, venerabiles patres infrascripti provincie Bituricensis personaliter et procuratores quorumdam absentium, videlicet (i) dominus Aymiunus abbas monasterii Case Dei⁹⁰ Claromontensis diocesis pro se et suo conventu et pro omnibus prioribus et officiariis omnium domorum prioratuum et monasteriorum dicte provincie ad eum et dictum monasterium suum et eiusdem monasterii conventum spectantium, necnon et pro omnibus prioribus et officiariis omnium domorum prioratuum et monasteriorum diocesis Aniciensis ad eundem dominum abbatem et dictum monasterium suum et eiusdem monasterii conventum spectantium, (ii) fratres Gaufridus de Fortio infirmarius et Arbertus Lupi monachus monasterii Dolensis⁹¹ pro abbate et conventu eiusdem monasterii et pro omnibus officiariis et menbris eorumdem de provincia predicta ut procuratores seu sindici eorumdem, (iii) dominus A. abbas monasterii de Aureliaco⁹² eiusdem diocesis pro se et suo conventu et pro omnibus officiariis prioribus domibus et menbris suis de eadem provincia, (iv) dominus .. abbas monasterii de Galhac⁹³ Albiensis diocesis pro se et suo conventu et pro omnibus officiariis prioribus domibus et menbris suis de provincia antedicta, (v) prior de Sancto Bricio⁹⁴ Bituricensis diocesis pro .. abbate Sancti Benedicti Floriacensis⁹⁵ ratione domus de Castellione⁹⁶ quam habet in diocese Bituricense ut procurator ipsius, (vi) frater G. de Pestel monachus monasterii Sancte Fidis de Conchas⁹⁷ Ruthenensis diocesis pro .. abbate et conventu eiusdem monasterii et pro omnibus officiariis prioribus domibus et menbris suis de

---

⁹⁰La Chaise-Dieu (Haute-Loire, cant. de Brioude).

⁹¹Déols (Indre, cant. de Châteauroux).

⁹²Aurillac (Cantal, ch.-l. de dép.).

⁹³Gaillac (Tarn, cant.).

⁹⁴St-Brisson-sur-Loire (Loiret, cant. de Gien).

⁹⁵St-Benoît-sur-Loire *alias* Fleury, diocese of Orléans (Loiret, cant. d'Ouzouer-sur-Loire).

⁹⁶Châtillon-sur-Loire (Loiret, cant.).

⁹⁷Conques (Aveyron, cant.).

dicta provincia ut procurator seu sindicus eorumdem, (vii) magister Durandus Messerii clericus pro abbate et conventu Vabren'[98] ordinis sancti Benedicti Ruthenensis diocesis et pro omnibus officiariis prioribus domibus et menbris ipsorum de dicta provincia ut procurator seu sindicus eorumdem, (viii) frater Raymundus Jaucerandi monachus monasterii Sancti de Theofredi[99] Aniciensis pro abbate et conventu eiusdem monasterii et pro omnibus officiariis prioribus domibus et menbris ipsorum de dicta provincia ut procurator et sindicus eorumdem, (ix) frater Rotbertus de Monasterio monachus Massiliensis pro abbate et conventu monasterii de Castris[100] Albiensis diocesis et pro omnibus officiariis prioratibus domibus et menbris ipsorum ut procurator seu sindicus eorumdem, (x) item prior prioratus de Capella Aude[101] Bituricensis diocesis ad abbatiam Sancti Dyonisii in Francia pertinentis personaliter pro se ipso, (xi) prior prioratus de Rulhiaco[102] Bituricensis diocesis ad eamdem abbatiam Sancti Dyonisii pertinentis personaliter pro se ipso, (xii) prior prioratus de Castro Novo supra Krum[103] eiusdem diocesis ad abbatiam Sancti Benedicti Floriacensis pertinentis personaliter pro se ipso, (xiii) prior prioratus de Sancto Bricio eiusdem diocesis ad eamdem abbatiam Sancti Benedicti pertinentis personaliter pro se ipso et nomine procuratorio et tanquam procurator prioris prioratus de Sancero[104] eiusdem diocesis et ad eamdem abbatiam Sancti Benedicti pertinentis et nomine procuratorio et tanquam procurator prioris de Monesterello[105] eiusdem diocesis et ad eamdem abbatiam pertinentis, (xiv) prior prioratus Sancti Desiderati[106] Bituricensis diocesis predicte ad abbatiam Sancti Michaelis de Clusa[107] pertinentis personaliter pro se ipso, (xv) prior prioratus de Glatinhiaco[108] eiusdem diocesis ad abbatiam Fontis Ebraud'[109] pertinentis personaliter pro se ipso et nomine

---

[98]Vabres (Aveyron, cant. de St-Affrique).

[99]St-Chaffre *alias* Le Monastier (Haute-Loire, cant. du Monastier-sur-Gazeille).

[100]Castres (Tarn, ch.-l. d'arr.).

[101]La Chapelaude (Allier, cant. d'Huriel).

[102]Reuilly (Indre, cant. d'Issoudun-nord).

[103]Châteauneuf-sur-Cher (Cher, cant.).

[104]Sancerre (Cher, cant.).

[105]Ménétréol-sur-Sauldre (Cher, cant. d'Aubigny-sur-Nère).

[106]St-Désiré (Allier, cant. d'Huriel).

[107]Chiusa di San Michele (St-Michel de Cluse), diocese of Turin, Piédmont.

[108]Glatigny (Indre, cant. de St-Christophe-en-Bazelle, com. de Chabris).

[109]Fontevrault, diocese of Poitiers (Maine-et-Loire, cant. de Saumur-sud).

procuratorio et tanquam sindicus seu procurator abbatisse et conventus Fontis Ebraudi ratione prioratuum et menbrorum omnium que habent in dicta provincia Bituricensis, (xvi) Johannes Blondelli de Virsione pro priorissa et conventu prioratus de Moneston super Krum[110] eiusdem diocesis et pro omnibus menbris suis ut procurator seu sindicus eorundem, (xvii) frater Bernardus de Servant monachus monasterii de Monteto[111] eiusdem diocesis pro priore prioratus eiusdem loci ad abbatiam Sancti Michaelis de Clusa pertinentis et pro omnibus menbris ipsius prioratus ut procurator seu syndicus prioris eiusdem, (xviii) prior de Sancto Bricio predictus pro capiterio et capitulo Sancti Martini Leriacen'[112] eiusdem diocesis ut procurator seu sindicus eorumdem, (xix) frater Gaufridus Belleti monachus monasterii de Sancto Porciano[113] Claromontensis diocesis pro priore et conventu ipsius monasterii et pro omnibus menbris suis ut procurator et sindicus eorumdem, (xx) prior Sancti Germani de Salis[114] eiusdem Claronmontensis diocesis ad abbatiam Virzilliacen'[115] pertinentis personaliter pro se ipso, (xxi) prior prioratus Sancte Marie[116] Cartusiensis ordinis eiusdem diocesis personaliter pro se ipso, (xxii) frater Guillelmus de Claveriis prior prioratus de Burgo[117] ad abbatiam de Aureliaco eiusdem diocesis pertinentis personaliter pro se ipso, (xxiii) prior prioratus de Salviaco[118] eiusdem diocesis ad abbatiam Sancti Michaelis de Clusa pertinentis personaliter pro se et conventu suo et omnibus menbris suis, (xxiv) prior prioratus Pontis Raterii[119] eiusdem diocesis ad predictam abbatiam Fontis Ebraudi pertinentis personaliter pro se ipso, (xxv) Durandus de Campo Bono clericus pro priore prioratuum de Ruinis[120] et de Menerie[121] eiusdem diocesis ad abbatiam monasterii Sancti Victoris

---

[110]Mennetou-sur-Cher (Loir-et-Cher, cant.).

[111]Le Montet (Allier, cant.).

[112]Léré (Cher, cant.).

[113]St-Pourçain-sur-Sioule (Allier, cant.).

[114]St-Germain-de-Salles (Allier, cant. de Chantelle).

[115]Vézelay, diocese of Autun (Yonne, cant.).

[116]Port-Sainte-Marie *alias* La Chartreuse (Puy-de-Dôme, cant. de Pontgibaud).

[117]Le Bourg (Lot, cant. Lacapelle-Marival).

[118]Sauviat (Puy-de-Dôme, cant. de Courpière).

[119]Pontratier (Allier, cant. de Gannat, com. de Charmes).

[120]Ruines (Cantal, cant. de Ruynes-en-Margeride).

[121]Mentières (Cantal, cant. de St-Flour-nord).

Massiliensis[122] pertinentium ut procurator prioris eiusdem, (xxvi) dominus Guillelmus Rotlandi prior prioratus de Dauzaco[123] eiusdem diocesis ad supradictam abbatiam de Aureliaco pertinentis personaliter pro se ipso et tanquam procurator prioris de Esparssac[124] eiusdem diocesis et ad eamdem abbatiam pertinentis, (xxvii) prior prioratus Sancti Johannis de Vendat[125] eiusdem diocesis ad predictam abbatiam Virzilliacen' pertinentis personaliter pro se ipso, (xxviii) frater Guillelmus de Chamboat monachus monasterii Portus Dei[126] pro priorissa et conventu Sancti Genesii prope Hermentum[127] eiusdem diocesis ut procurator seu sindicus earumdem et pro omnibus menbris suis, (xxix) Johannes Dalamanssas pro priorissa et conventu monasterii de Comps[128] eiusdem diocesis et omnibus menbris suis ut procurator seu sindicus earumdem, (xxx) Philippus de Rocolis canonicus ecclesie Brivaten'[129] eiusdem diocesis pro proposito decano et sacrista ipsius ecclesie, (xxxi) Bertrandus Vero de Area eiusdem ecclesie canonicus pro capitulo ipsius ecclesie, ut procuratores seu sindici eorumdem, (xxxii) Marchus de Sancto Ylario clericus pro prioribus prioratuum de Godeto,[130] de Volta,[131] Belliloci,[132] de Chaspinhac[133] et de Prahalhas[134] ordinis sancti Benedicti Aniciensis diocesis ut procurator seu sindicus eorumdem, (xxxii) dominus Hugo Dalcher canonicus Sancti Georgii de Sancto Pauliano[135] pro priore de Landoas[136] eiusdem Aniciensis diocesis ut procurator ipsius, (xxxiii) prior

---

[122]Marseilles, province of Arles (Bouches-du-Rhône, ch.-l. de dép.).

[123]Dauzat-sur-Vodable (Puy-de-Dôme, cant. d'Ardes).

[124]Probably a scribal error for 'de Jussaco': Jussac (Cantal, cant. d'Aurillac-sud).

[125]Vendat (Allier, cant. d'Escurolles).

[126]Port-Dieu (Corrèze, cant. de Bort-les-Orgues).

[127]St-Genès-les-Monges (Puy-de-Dôme, cant. de Pontaumur, com. de Puy-St-Gulmier).

[128]Comps, *later* Lavaudieu (Haute-Loire, cant. de Brioude).

[129]Brioude (Haute-Loire, ch.-l. d'arr.).

[130]Goudet (Haute-Loire, cant. du Monastier-sur-Gazeille).

[131]Lavoûte-sur-Loire (Haute-Loire, cant. de St-Paulien).

[132]Beaulieu (Haute-Loire, cant. de Vorey).

[133]Chaspinhac (Haute-Loire, cant. du Puy-nord).

[134]Présailles (Haute-Loire, cant. du Monastier-sur-Gazeille).

[135]St-Georges à St-Paulien (Haute-Loire, cant.).

[136]Landos (Haute-Loire, cant. de Pradelles).

prioratus de Auriaco[137] eiusdem diocesis ad dictam abbatiam Sancti Michaelis de Clusa pertinentis pro se, (xxxiv) item prior prioratus de Cumiliaco[138] Claromontensis diocesis ad eamdem abbatiam Sancti Michaelis pertinentis pro se et conventu suo et omnibus menbris suis, (xxxv) item prior prioratus Sancti Laurentii prope Sanctum Leontium[139] Ruthenensis diocesis ad abbatiam Massilien' predictam pertinentis pro se et pro prioribus prioratuum Sancti Amantii burgi Ruthen',[140] Sancti Leontii,[141] Sancti Stephani prope Amiliavum,[142] de Castro Novo,[143] de la Verana,[144] de Amiliano[145] et Sancti Genesii de Rippa Olti[146] eiusdem diocesis et ad eamdem abbatiam pertinentium, item et pro prioribus prioratuum de Canonica[147] Mimatensis diocesis et de Ambileto[148] Albiensis diocesis ad eamdem abbatiam pertinentium et pro prioribus Sancti Petri de Altesio[149] et de Petra Mala[150] eiusdem diocesis ut procurator seu sindicus eorumdem, (xxxvi) dominus Bonuspar Lordeti prior prioratus monasterii de Chiriaco[151] Mimatensis diocesis ad dictam abbatiam Massilien' et prioratus de Floriaco[152] eiusdem diocesis ad abbatiam Case Dei et prioratus de Podio Celsi[153] Albiensis diocesis ad dictam abbatiam de Aureliaco pertinentium personaliter pro se et tanquam procurator

---

[137]Aurec-sur-Loire (Haute-Loire, cant.).

[138]Cunlhat (Puy-de-Dôme, cant.).

[139]St-Laurent-de-Lévézou, near St-Léons (Aveyron, cant. de Vézins-de-Lévézou).

[140]St-Amans Rodez (Aveyron, ch.-l. d'arr.).

[141]St-Léons (Aveyron, cant. de Vézins-de-Lévézou).

[142]St-Etienne (Aveyron, com. de Millau).

[143]Castelnau-Pégayrols (Aveyron, cant. de Beauzély).

[144]Lavernhe (Aveyron, cant. de Sévérac-le-Château).

[145]Millau (Aveyron, ch.-l. d'arr.).

[146]St-Geniez-d'Olt (Aveyron, cant.).

[147]La Canourgue (Lozère, cant.).

[148]Ambialet (Tarn, cant. de Villefranche-d'Albigeois).

[149]Altès (Aveyron, cant. de Sévérac-le-Château).

[150]Lapeyre (Aveyron, cant. de St-Affrique, com. de Versols-et-Lapeyre).

[151]Chirac (Lozère, cant. de St-Germain-du-Teil).

[152]Florac (Lozère, ch.-l. d'arr.).

[153]Puycelci (Tarn, cant. de Castelnau de Montmiral).

prioratuum de Espanhac[154] dicte Mimatensis diocesis ad dictam abbatiam de Aureliaco et de Prevencheriis[155] eiusdem diocesis ad abbatiam Sancti Egidii in Provincia[156] pertinentium et nomine procuratorio eorumdem, (xxxvii) magister Raymundus de Longodosco clericus pro priore et conventu monasterii Sancti Anthonini[157] et pro omnibus menbris et subditis suis ut procurator eorum qui sunt de diocese Ruthenense, (xxxviii) magister Durandus Messerii clericus pro prioribus prioratuum de Brusca[158] et Sancti Crespini[159] eiusdem diocesis ad monasterium Sancti Pontii de Tomeriis[160] pertinentium ut procurator eorum, (xxxix) P. Sessaudi clericus pro priore de Bobonio[161] Lemovicensis diocesis ordinis Fontis Ebraud'. Omnes inquam prenominati nona die dicti mensis in crastinum dicte octave diei (*9 November 1294*) coram prenominatis clericis dicti domini regis in capitulo fratrum predicatorum Clarom' comparentes, unanimiter et concorditer deliberato concilio requisitione eis facta per dictos clericos dicti domini regis super dicta subventione domino regi facienda et expositis eis causis et rationibus prout decuit obtulerunt sponte et gratiose et sua bona et mera liberalitate eisdem clericis domini regis pro ipso domino rege recipientibus decimam suorum reddituum ecclesiasticorum que habent in regno Francie, ad tempus et modis et formis ac conditionibus quibus prelati et alii ordinarii eiusdem provincie Bituricensis in concilio apud Aureliacum Claromontensis diocesis per officialem Bituricensem cum suffraganeis dicte provincie domino Bituricense archiepiscopo in remotis agente pridie celebrato concesserunt domino regi. Et religiosum virum dominum Bonumpar Lordeti supradictum priorem monasterii de Chiriaco dicte diocesis Mimatensis concorditer constituerunt et deputaverunt generalem levatorem et collectorem huiusmodi decime solvende dicto domino nostro regi, ita tamen quod ipse prior in qualibet diocese dicte provincie loco sui possit unum vel plures collectores dicte decime substituere et deputare prout et de quibus sibi placuerit et videbitur faciendum. Acta fuerunt hec in supradicto capitulo anno indictione mense et nona die antedictis (*9 November 1294*) presentibus nobilibus viris domino Guillelmo Aycellini

---

[154]Ispagnac (Lozère, cant. de Florac).

[155]Prévenchères (Lozère, cant. de Villefort).

[156]St-Gilles, diocese of Nîmes (Gard, cant.).

[157]St-Antonin (Tarn-et-Garonne, cant. de St-Antonin-Noble-Val).

[158]Brusque (Aveyron, cant. de Camarès).

[159]St-Crépin (Aveyron, cant. de St-Sernin-sur-Rance, com. de Laval-Roquecezière).

[160]St-Pons-de-Thomières, diocese of Narbonne (Hérault, cant.).

[161]Boubon (Haute-Vienne, cant. d'Oradour-sur-Vayre, com. de Cussac).

milite tenente locum ballivi Arvernie in eius absentia et dominis G. de Peyrussa, Audino Chauleri et Ademaro de Nova Villa militibus, magistro Petro de Monjou canonico Laudun' et pluribus aliis clericis et laicis testibus ad premissa vocatis specialiter et rogatis. Et ego Johannes Renulphi de Ussello Limovicensis diocesis auctoritate sacrosancte Romane ecclesie notarius publicus premissis omnibus et singulis vocatus et rogatus unacum predictis testibus presens interfui et ea omnia prout supra leguntur ad requisitionem predictorum clericorum dicti domini regis et de mandato dictorum concedentium propria manu fideliter scripsi publicavi et in hanc publicam formam redegi meoque consueto signo signavi.

Appendix C.   ASSEMBLY OF THE ABBOTS AND PRIORS OF THE ORDER OF CLUNY AT SENS SHORTLY BEFORE 3 OCTOBER 1294

The place and date of the assembly are from 1 below. In the case of the abbey of Moissac, in the diocese of Cahors, there was a disputed abbatial election (see Gallia Christiana in provincias ecclesiasticas distributa (16 vols, Paris, 1715-1865), 1, p. 169) and the concession of a subsidy (in fact to the value of a quadrennial tenth) by proctors appointed by the convent was not made until 30 October 1295: see AN J1035 no. 40 (letter of proxy) and no. 40 bis (grant of subsidy).

1   Grant of biennial tenth

Printed from the original: AN J259 Cluny no. 3 (32 cm. X 25 cm. plus 2 cm. (pli); seal tag and seal; dorse in contemporary hand 'littere abbatis Cluniacensis pro subventione concessa domino regi'. The edition of the same source in Recueil des chartes de l'abbaye de Cluny. ed. Auguste-Joseph BERNARD & Alexandre BRUEL, Paris, 1876-1903, 6, no. 5401, omits the long and interesting preamble.

Universis presentes literas inspecturis frater Guillelmus miseratione divina Cluniacensis ecclesie minister humilis salutem in domino. Quanto studio et quam ferventi desiderio serenissimus princeps noster et dominus Philippus dei gratia Francorum rex et incliti progenitores eiusdem deffensionis clipei et salutis causam illius, qui pro salute populi in ara crucis se ipsum obtulit hostiam deo patri, susceperint, et pro reverentia crucifixi cuius se semper obsequiis ascripsuerint, continuata devotione univerint finem principio, adeo etiam et in tantum quod toto tempore vite sue toti fuerint ecclesie toti dei, ita quod apud altissimum quicquid est integritatis servarunt et apud homines nil expositionis notabilis incurrerunt, novit deus Romana mater ecclesia et tota universitas Christiana. Propter que et non immerito ipsius et sui regni periculum et offensa universalem ecclesiam non pretereunt inoffensam, quin immo tam cari principis petitio seu causa non est contemptui exponenda, presertim cum ex ipsius favore et gratia multipliciter possit et valeat utilitatibus ecclesiarum accresci tum in conservatione quietis tum in promotione negotiorum que apud ipsum promovenda pro tempore imminebunt. Horum profecto consideratio nostrum et aliorum .. abbatum nostri ordinis et priorum nuper apud Senonis propter hoc vocatorum interpellavit affectum ut reverentiam ad ipsum que tantum decet principem studeamus habere ipsumque ad deffensionem regni Francie et corone contra hostes eiusdem, qui ad fallaces recurrentes versutias in regni dispendium corda multorum nituntur evertere et eorum retibus implicare prout refertur communiter a plerisque, gratiose et liberaliter adiuvare, ut extunc rex tam grandis et fortis cause dei et ecclesie prout dictum est superius hactenus prosecutor et totius Christianitatis athleta potenter aggrediatur tam grande negotium, et, prout melius poterit et debebit, partem concurrat[162] et refrenet ab insultibus malivolis et malignis adversam, ut per hoc divino adiutorio mediante in dicto regno et sub ipsius regimine more solito habeantur tempora pacifica et tranquilla. Eapropter deliberatione provida cum .. abbatibus et prioribus antedictis ad supportanda per dictum principem nostrum levius supradicta, duximus ordinandum quod (i) unaquaque ordinis nostri persona, que olim decimam solvere consuevit, in valore et quantitate decime iuxta declarationem et taxationem hactenus habitas per Romanam ecclesiam vel per legatum eiusdem, de redditibus dicti ordinis in regno Francie constitutis eidem domino regi ad biennium subveniat gratiose (ii) et per aliquos de dicto ordine collectores, per nos et non per alium assumendos, dicta quantitas levabitur et in qualibet dicti ordinis cameraria dicti domini regis gentibus per eosdem collectores deliberabitur et tradetur ad terminos infrascriptos, (iii) videlicet pro primo anno medietas ipsius quantitatis die dominica qua cantatur Letare Hierusalem (*13 March 1295*) et alia medietas in subsequenti festo beati Michaelis (*29 September*). In secundo anno et pro secundo anno fiet solutio et satisfactio eodem modo et eisdem festivitatibus et terminis quibus supra. (iv) Et si aliquis de dicto ordine aliquo de statutis terminis in toto vel in parte deficeret in solvendo, ad ipsum defficientem, non ad nos, non ad quemquam alium de dicto ordine per dictum dominum vel suos pro defectu solutionis huiusmodi haberetur recursus. (v) Si tamen Romana ecclesia citra et infra dictum biennium eidem domino regi vel alii cuicumque decimam a nobis et a personis dicti ordinis exigendam concederet aut levandam vel fuerit iam concessa aut sibimet eadem ecclesia pro supportandis vel faciendis aliquibus retineret vel per eam fuerit iam retenta, nos et persone predicte nullatenus teneremur ad quantitatem predictam. Id idem esset et fieret, si maius quam sit decima eadem ecclesia nobis et dicto ordini citra dictum biennium imponeret, aut iam sic impositum in presenti. Quod si, citra dictum biennium, minorem partem quam sit decima supradicta imponeret aut iam nobis et dicto ordini imposita reperiatur a casu, illud sic impositum deduceretur de quantitate predicta. (vi) Si vero citra biennium antedictum fieret, quod concedat altissimus, pax et concordia et cessaret impugnatio dicti regni, cessaret extunc similiter solutio quantitatis predicte, nec ad ipsam nos et persone dicti ordinis aliquatenus teneremur. Et si interim treuga iniretur, ad solvendum

---

[162]concurrat *in a fold and difficult to read.*

quantitatem huiusmodi nos et ordo minime teneremur durante treuga supradicta. (vii) Et hec cum dictis abbatibus et prioribus ordinavimus facienda modis et conditionibus infrascriptis, videlicet quod per subventionem huiusmodi nullum ius in possesione vel in proprietate contra nos et dictum ordinem, necnon et contra privilegia et libertates dicti ordinis, in casu simili vel dissimili, dicto domino regi aut suis successoribus acquiratur de novo et quod nullum fiat nobis preiudicium in futurum. (viii) Iterum quod dictus dominus rex vel sui, durante dicto biennio, a nobis et personis, familia et hominibus dicti ordinis nullam aliam subventionem seu prestationem aut servitium aliud quodlibet et quodcumque in rebus propriis vel personis occasione dissensionis et neccessitatis huiusmodi possit aut valeat exigere, petere etiam vel levare, rursusque nulli duces, comites, barones, castellani et alii domini quilibet et quicumque, quocumque nomine censeantur, a nobis et dicto ordine, personis et familia et hominibus dicti ordinis occasione dissensionis et neccessitatis huiusmodi, pro quibus dictus dominus rex subventionem habet predictam, vel per se vel per alios possint exigere vel levare, vel eos in personis vel rebus afficere, gravare, cogere, onerare, aut alias opprimere quoquomodo, et si contrarium eveniret, quod dictus dominus rex nos et eos deffenderet a predictis et amoveret predicta. In quorum omnium testimonium presentibus litteris sigillum nostrum duximus apponendum. Datum die dominica post festum beati Michaelis anno domini millesimo ducentesimo nonagesimo quarto. (*3 October 1294*)

2   Royal acceptance of the tenth

Printed here from AN J938 no. 38, which is a draft copy with corrections. The corrected sections are in italics in the text below. It is also printed in BERNARD & BRUEL (see p. 46), 6, no. 5402.

Philippus .. dei gratia Franc' .. rex universis presentes litteras inspecturis salutem. Noverit universitas .. vestra quod cum religiosi viri .. abbas Clugniacensis ceterique abbates et priores Clugniacensis ordinis dilecti nostri, nuper Senonas propter hoc specialiter evocati, decimam omnem ecclesiasticorum proventuum suorum nobis in subsidium pro defensione et felici statu regni nostri et pro reprimendis emulorum et inimicorum eiusdem regni, nostram et ipsius transquillitatem et pacem turbare satagentium, hostilibus impugnationibus nobis ad byennium integrum sub certis modis et conditionibus concesserint graciose, prout in patentibus ipsius .. abbatis litteris inde confectis plenius continetur, hoc expresse adiecto in conditionibus antedictis, quod *nos aut* duces .. comites .. barones .. castellani et alii domini nostro subiecti dominio, quicumcue sint et cuiuscumque conditionis existant, a dictis .. abbatibus prioribus personis familia et hominibus *ac hospitibus* dicti ordinis, occasione impugnationum et defensionis huiusmodi pro quibus religiosi prefati subventionum huiusmodi nobis prestant, *nullam aliam subventionem per viam doni seu mutui aut alicuius cuiuslibet extraordinarie exactionis* valeamus aut levare, salvis tamen antiquis iuribus vel *deveriis et servitiis ordinariis nostris et dominorum ipsorum in casibus consuetis*, in personis aut rebus propter hoc molestari offendi gravari vel alias opprimi *nequeant*, nosque huiusmodi gravamina, si eis occasione huiusmodi inferrentur, submovere curabimus et ipsos ab huiusmodi gravaminibus defendere et tueri. Nos huiusmodi decimam ab ipsis oblatam nobis taliter et concessam, sub modis et conditionibus antedictis, tenore presentium acceptamus, modos et conditiones eosdem volentes laudentes et approbantes expresse, nolentes nec intendentes hoc ad consequentiam trahi vel abbatibus prioribus et ordini supradictis aliquam per hoc novitatem induci vel preiudicium generari. In cuius rei testimonium presentibus litteris nostrum fecimus apponi sigillum. Actum Parisius die lune in festo beati Luce evangeliste anno domini m° cc° nonagesimo quarto. (*18 October 1294*)

Appendix D. COUNCIL OF THE PROVINCE OF TOURS AT SAUMUR, 3-5 OCTOBER 1294

For the date of the council see 1 below. A set of detailed and extremely forthright complaints against the activities of royal officials was addressed to the king at about the time of the council by Guillaume le Maire, bishop of Angers. They were in the form of grievances from this individual bishop, and he included a copy of the grievances in his Liber (PORT (see n. 25), pp. 322-31) immediately preceding a copy of the letter printed below (2) conceding a grant to the king. There is a possibility, though it can be put no stronger, that the complaints were linked with the work of the provincial council. The council was not just concerned with the call to aid the king, for the archbishop of Tours issued there five reforming canons, dated 5 October (see 1 below). The preface to these canons declares that the council, to which the suffragan bishops, chapters, abbots and others had been summoned, took place between Sunday 3 October and Tuesday 5 October. The grant to the king (2) survives in two versions. The version entered by the bishop of Angers into his Liber is the *actum* as drawn up in the council on 5 October and dated and sealed later by the bishop himself, perhaps the Saturday following, i.e. 9 October (see below p. 53 n. 202). The *actum* is the concession by the archbishop and bishops of the province. It may have been left to each bishop to send a letter of concession to the king, either by sealing the *actum* or by re-drafting it, for the second version of the grant, as printed here, is the bishop of St-Pol-de-Léon's letter, the text of which varies, but not substantially, from the *actum*.

1 Statutes published at the Council

Five reforming canons were published concerning the correct dress of monks, the procedure for the absolution from excommunication of the dying, the wrongful activities of archdeacons and lesser officials in exacting fines for sins and in sending out clerks to hear confessions, and the attacks upon tithes of those exercising temporal authority. They are printed in AVRIL (see n. 1), pp. 302-6, Jean MAAN, Sancta et metropolitana ecclesia Turonensis, Tours, 1667, pt ii. 70-1, LABBE & COSSART (see n. 5), 11, pt ii. 1395-7, HARDOUIN (see n. 5), 7, col. 1169-72, COLETI (see n. 5), 14, col. 1211 and MANSI (see n. 5), 24, col. 1121-4. In HEFELE-LECLERCQ (see n. 5), 6, pt i, pp. 345-6 and in AVRIL the council and the canons are ascribed to May 1294 through a confusion of two feast days of Michael the Archangel (8 May and 29 Sept.). The second of these is apparently the one referred to, for the dating clause of the letter edited here (below p. 00 n. 000), which relates to the council which must have been held in the autumn of 1294 (the earliest summons for all these councils is 31 July, see A1), is precisely the same as the dating clause of the canons.

2   Grant of biennial tenth

Printed here from AN J1035 no. 39 (=A): 28 cm. X 36 cm., tongue for seal torn away; on dorse in contemporary hand 'littere super concessione biennalis decime in dyocesi Leonensi'. This text is collated here with the *actum* in the book of the bishop of Angers (PORT (see n. 25), pp. 320-2 and AVRIL (see n. 1), pp. 309-12), which has been checked with the manuscript, that is AD Maine-et-Loire, G7, fos. 52v-54r (=B). Bibliothèque Municipale Nantes, MS 36, fos. 280r-281r is an eighteenth-century copy of the same text as B: see AVRIL, pp. 41-2, 309.

Universis Christi fidelibus presentes litteras inspecturis .. Guillelmus permissione divina episcopus Leonensis salutem in domino. Extollenda[163] dignis laudum preconiis benedicti regni Francorum mira devotio ineffabilisque regum eiusdem regni benignitatis ac liberalitatis in ecclesias munificentia clerum regni memorati ac omnem ecclesiasticum ordinem naturalis rationis instinctu provocat et inducit ipsum regnum prosequi sincere[164] caritatis affectu, eidem cura vigilantiori consulere, eiusdem necessitatibus[165] non tantum orationum suffragiis sed etiam bonorum temporalium subsidiis conditione temporis exigente liberaliter[166] subvenire. Ipsum nempe[167] regnum, pre regnis ceteris ubicumque[168] terrarum longe lateque diffusis, semper sacre religionis extitit fundamentum, columpna et scutum ecclesie, tutamentum fidei, fons sapientie irrigans totum orbem fluentis plenissimis scripturarum, cuius etiam principes videlicet Christianissimi Francorum reges, pre cunctis terre regibus, puriori fidei lumine radiantes, fundaverunt monasteria, mirifice dotaverunt ecclesias[169] multiplicibus immunitatum ac libertatum[170] privilegiorumque insigniis decorando, et quia semper pre cunctis terre pincipibus deo et ecclesie devoti et humiles perstiterunt, deum pie colendo, ecclesias et ecclesie ministros sicut decet principem Christianum devotius[171] honorando, gloriosus princeps regum terre per quem ceteri reges regnant eis recompensavit[172] in hac vita regnum Francorum per feliciora successivis temporibus

---

[163]B *begins* Extollenda... *following the heading* Littera gratie domino regi concesse in concilio Salmuriensi.

[164]sincero B.

[165]necessitatis A.

[166]liberalitat' A.

[167]nampe B.

[168]ubique B.

[169]*add* eas B.

[170]liberalitatum A.

[171]diutius A.

[172]*add* etiam B.

incrementa super omnia regnorum climata sublimando, eisdem[173]
victoriam et triumphum de hostibus largiendo,[174] terrasque ipsorum
hostium in ipsos sua irrefragabili potentia transferendo. Cum itaque quidam
iniquitatis filii, totius Christianitatis ac catholice fidei turbatores, quorum rex
Anglorum, ore vulgi celebrante ac fama celebri refferente, noscitur esse
capud, regni memorati felicibus prosperitatis proventibus invidentes, ac
venenum quod diutius[175] venenatis visceribus latuit modernis temporibus
evomentes, ipsum regnum multifariis conspirationum et coniurationum
factionibus adhibitis impugnare et subvertere presumptione dampnabili
molliuntur, iam in diversa[176] ipsius regni loca insanienti furia hostiliter
irruentes, quorum perversis ac virosis machinationibus,[177] nisi maturius
obvietur eorum callidam et subdolam dementiam armorum potentia
repulsando, ipsi regno et eius habitatoribus non tantum laicis sed etiam
clericis ac ecclesiis universis posset grave periculum imminere.
Quocirca[178] neccessitatem regni ac ecclesiarum eiusdem pariter
attendentes, illustrissimo domino Philippo Francorum regi ob
defensionem[179] regni ac ecclesiarum[180] nimiis expensarum oneribus
pregravato, ad que onera supportanda sine regnicolarum ac ecclesiarum
subsidio proprie non sufficerent facultates, pro nostre modulo
potestatis[181] dignum duximus succurrendum. (i) Concedimus itaque dicto
domino regi hac vice communi consensu cleri nostri, in[182] provinciali
concilio apud Salmurum nuper celebrato congregati et procuratorum
absentium,[183] super hoc accedente ob neccessitatem dicti regni, ut
premittitur, verisimiliter imminentem et propter deffensionem et tuitionem
regni ecclesiarum et personarum ecclesiaticarum et bonorum earumdem, una
cum aliis ecclesie Britannie episcopis,[184] de bonis mobilibus nostris[185]

---

[173]eosdem A.

[174]largiando A.

[175]diu est A.

[176]diversi A.

[177]*omit* machinationibus A.

[178]*add* nos B.

[179]*add* dicti B.

[180]*add* eiusdem B.

[181]de bonis nostris mobilibus *instead of* pro ... potestatis B.

[182]*add* nostro B.

[183]*omit* et ... absentium B.

[184]*omit* una ... episcopis B.

et personarum ecclesiasticarum nostrarum civitatis et[186] diocesum non
exemptarum dumtaxat usque ad biennium tantam pecunie summam, quantam
a nobis et aliis personis ecclesiasticis predictis nomine decime pro tempore
quo decimam habebat ex concessione sancte Romane ecclesie deductis
sumptibus percipere consuevit ad antiquam taxationem salvis antiquis
libertatibus et franchisiis ecclesie nostre,[187] (ii) ita tamen quod per istam
concessiionem nullum preiudicium ecclesiis nobis et aliis personis
ecclesiasticis generetur nec aliqua servitus[188] in predictis ecclesiis
acquiratur et quod (iii) si[189] durante tempore concessionis predicte
decimam seu maius onus aut simile in eodem regno per sedem apostolicam
concedi vel imponi contingerit (*sic*) vel iam etiam sit concessum seu (iv)
domino inspirante cui non est difficile diiuncta coniungere pax inter dictos
reges durante dicto biennio reformetur, ex toto[190] cessabitur a solutione
concessionis predicte.[191] (v) Si vero dicto tempore treugam inter dictos
reges iniri contingerit (*sic*), pro illo tempore quo treuga duraverit antedicta
huius concessionis prestatio[192] totaliter suspendetur, et (vi) si duces
comites aut barones dicti regni[193] vellent durante dicto tempore aliquam
subventionem vel subsidium[194] ab ecclesiis et personis ecclesiasticis[195]
exigere vel habere, dominus rex faceret ipsos cessare cum effectu. (vii) Et
colligetur dicta summa per illos quos nos in nostris civitate et diocesi[196]
ad hec duxerimus[197] deputandos, terminis infrascriptis, ita quod
medietatem in instanti festo nativitatis beati Johannis baptiste[198] (*24 June*)
et aliam medietatem in festo Omnium Sanctorum (*1 November*) postea

---

[185]de ... nostris *omitted in* A *but required by the sense.*

[186]*omit* civitatis et B.

[187]*omit* ad antiquam ... ecclesie nostre B.

[188]*add* domino regi B.

[189]*omit* si A.

[190]tunc B.

[191]supradicte B.

[192]*add* ex tunc B.

[193]dictarum dyocesum *instead of* dicti regni B.

[194]*add* non debitum B.

[195]*add* predictis B.

[196]predicti archiepiscopus et episcopus quilibet in sua dyocesi *instead of* in ... diocesi B.

[197]deduximus A.

[198]resurrectionis dominice (*3 April 1295*) *instead of* nativitatis ... baptiste B.

subsequente, et eisdem terminis anni immediate sequentis prefatis receptoribus quilibet[199] modo quo supra solvere[200] teneatur. (viii) Et si forte aliqui in predictis terminis portionem ipsos contingentem solvere distulerint, ad id per censuram ecclesiasticam et aliter compellentur, nec iusticiarii seculares regales vel alii se ad hoc ullatenus intromittent, nisi a nobis vel a receptoribus super hoc a nobis deputandis specialiter fuerint requisiti, (ix) iidemque receptores peccuniam quam exinde[201] exegerint et receperint nobis tradent ut eam domino regi possimus postmodum assignare,[202] (x) ita nichilominus quod dictus dominus rex det nobis litteras suas sigillo suo sigillatas harum seriem continentes quod sub modo forma et conditionibus predictis huiusmodi subventionem seu subventionis concessionem acceptet. In quarum rerum testimonium presentes litteras fieri fecimus et sigilli nostri munimine roborari. Actum apud Salmurum Andegavensis diocesis die martis post festum beati Michaelis archangeli anno domini millesimo cc[o] nonagesimo quarto. (*5 October 1294*)

Appendix E.   COUNCIL OF THE PROVINCE OF RHEIMS AT COMPIEGNE, 5 OCTOBER 1294

The date of the grant of a subsidy (1 below) and the date of the precautionary appeal (2) indicate that the council was held on 5 October. The presence of the archbishop, Pierre Barbette, and of other prelates is referred to in 2, but it is not clear which of the suffragan bishops attended. Of the eleven suffragan bishoprics of the province it seems that only the see of Arras was vacant.[203] Whether or not the northern part of the province should respond to the king's request was, perhaps, initially in some question, for local 'temporal lords' had already sought, and to some extent obtained, financial assistance for the defence of the kingdom from those having benefices and ecclesiastical goods in the dioceses of Thérouanne, Arras and Tournai (3); and only part of the diocese of Cambrai lay within the kingdom of France.[204]

---

[199]quibus A.

[200]*omit* solvere A.

[201]inde B.

[202]*at this point* B *ends as follows*: Actum apud Salmurium durante predicto concilio provinciali die martis post festum beati Michaelis in Monte Gargano anno domino m[o] cc[o] nonagesimo quarto. (*5 October 1294*) Datum huius littere die sabbati et anno predicto. (*?9 October 1294*) In cuius rei testimonium sigillum nostrum presentibus litteris duximus apponendum.

[203]EUBEL (see n. 80), 1, pp. 11, 117: John the Monk was bishop-elect of Arras before he was made cardinal-priest of St Marcellinus and St Peter in Sept. 1294.

[204]See Recueil des historiens (see n. 16), 21, p. 541 and STRAYER, Philip the Fair (see n. 9), pp. 365-6.

1   **Grant of biennial tenth**
Printed from AN JJ34, fo. 49r-v (item 72).

Ad publicam mundi notitiam a prescis temporibus iam pervenit quod
benedictum regnum Francie pre ceteris mundi regnis hactenus extitit
ortodoxe fidei munimentum invincibile presidium catholice puritatis in quo
semper pax viguit fides crevit catholica et religio Christiana auctore domino
suscepit felicia incrementa. Nam sub protectione prescripti principis domini
regis nostri suorumque progenitorum regum Francie amotis offendiculis
gallicana fuit ecclesia in pacis pulcritudine et requie opulenta et illa mutua
caritate que inter personas ecclesiasticas principes et barones dicti regni
Francie concurrebat fruemur in posterum domino permittente. Attendentes
igitur quod rex Anglie ex concepta diu nequitia, ut rumor moscus enuntiat,
confederatus cum quibusdam magnis et potentibus extra regnum, quos ad
hoc muneribus et aliis diversis machinationibus callide noscitur induxisse,
sicut evidenter apparet, aspiret ad turbationem pacis in eodem regno et ad
impugnationem hostilem regis regnique sui suadente dyabolo, qui semper
satagit inter fratres discordiam seminare, prout eiusdem regis Anglie excessus
notorii manifesta facinora et execrabilia cognamina multipliciter detestantur,
et quia iacula que previdentur minus feriunt atque ledunt, vias exquirimus
ut idem rex noster et dominus regnumque suum et cohabitantes in eo ab
impugnationibus hostium securius valeat se tueri, si forte regem aut regnum
seu partem ipsius impugnari, quod absit, hostiliter contingeret quoquomodo,
nuper in Remensi provinciali concilio per nos archiepiscopum apud
Compendium propter hoc specialiter evocato diligenti deliberatione
prehabita providimus (i) fore subveniendum domino nostri regi ad nostram
et eiusdem regni defensionem, prout necessitas evidens id exposcit, partem
decimam omnium reddituum et proventuum ecclesiasticorum Remensis
provincie in regno Francie existentium propter dictam necessitatem
verisimiliter imminentem de consensu unanimi et concordi nostro et omnium
tunc inibi personaliter existentium necnon procuratorum personarum
absentium, sub certa forma quam sedes apostolica hactenus observavit, dicto
domino regi hac vice per biennium de speciali gratia concedentes quod per
unum canonicum cuiuslibet cathedralis ecclesie Remensis provincie et alium
virum ydoneum et discretum quos ad hoc quilibet episcopus in sua dyocese
deputaverit fideliter infrascriptis terminis colligetur, (ii) ita quod medietatem
ipsius in instante nativitatis domini (*25 December*) et aliam medietatem in
festo nativitatis sancti Johannis baptiste (*24 June*) postea subsequentis et
eisdem terminis anni immediate sequentis vice et nomine concilii prefatis
receptoribus quilibet modo quo supra solvere teneatur prefatis personis et
procuratoribus in hoc consentientibus penitus et expresse. (iii) Et si forte
aliqui in predictis terminis ipsam partem decimam solvere distulerunt, ad id
per censuram ecclesiasticam et aliter compellentur, nec regales de hoc se
ullatenus intromittent, nisi a receptoribus super hoc deputatis specialiter

fuerint evocati. (iv) Iidemque receptores pecuniam quam exinde exegerint et receperint in hac parte suo episcopo assignabunt ut eam domino regi valeant exhibere, (v) ita tamen quod si durante dicto biennio decimam seu maius onus aut simile in eodem regno per sedem apostolicam concedi vel imponi contigerit vel iam etiam sit concessum seu (vi) domino inspirante cui non est difficile disiuncta coniungere pax inter dictos reges durante dicto biennio reformetur ex toto cessabitur a solutione partis decime supradicte. (vii) Si vero dicto tempore treugam inter eosdem reges iniri contigerit pro illo tempore quo treuga duraverit antedicta huiusmodi solutio totaliter suspendetur. In cuius rei testimonium presentes litteras fieri fecimus et sigillorum nostrum munimine roborari. Datum et actum apud Compendium anno domini millesimo ducentesimo nonagesimo quarto die martis post festum beati Remigii. (*5 October 1294*)

2 **Precautionary appeal to Rome of the proctors of the cathedral churches of Rheims, Soissons, Châlons-sur-Marne, Laon, Senlis, Beauvais, Amiens, Noyon, Arras, Thérouanne, and Tournai, ratified by the dean and chapter of Laon**
Printed from the original notarial instrument, BN Picardie 284 no. 20 (27 cm. X 40 cm.) once in the archive of the cathedral church of Laon. Dorse: Cotté 49, 6e Layette; and in a later hand: Egl de Laon n. 94, 1294 7 Oct. A copy of this instrument or of a duplicate appears, with many errors of transcription, in BN Picardie 110, fos. 86r-87r.

In nomine domini nostri Jesu Christi Amen. Anno incarnationis eiusdem millesimo ducentesimo nonagesimo quarto septima die mensis Octobris indictione octava (*7 October 1294*) in presentia mei publici notarii et testium subscriptorum constituti venerabiles viri .. decanus et capitulum ecclesie Laudunensis in eorundem capitulo ad sonum campane more solito congregati asserentes procuratorem suum in provinciali concilio nuper apud Compendium celebrato provocasse seu appellasse ad sedem apostolicam, prout continetur in quadam cedula coram me notario et testibus subscriptis in dicto capitulo lecta, cuius tenor talis est: Nos procuratores cathedralium ecclesiarum Remensis provincie Cameracensi excepta coram vobis reverendis patribus .. domino Remensi archiepiscopo et ceteris dicimus et proponimus quod super subventione domino regi Francie facienda, de qua in vestro provinciali concilio tractabatur, nostram sub certis modo et forma et conditionibus vobis predictis reverendis patribus diximus et expressimus voluntatem et sub testimonio competenti multorum proborum et tabellionis publici super quibus factum est publicum instrumentum, a qua non intendimus recedere quoquo modo. Propter quod vobis attentius supplicamus ne contra nostram voluntatem predictam aliquid ordinetis statuatis seu etiam promulgetis, cui ordinationi statuto seu promulgationi si nostre voluntati predicte contrarietur in aliquo, quod absit, ex nunc nomine quo supra contradicimus et nos opponimus, de contradictione et oppositione nostris predictis et de non consensu instantium presentia publice protestantes ne tamen ad ordinationem statutum seu promulgationem que nostre voluntati predicte contrarientur in aliquo in predictarum ecclesiarum preiudicium seu gravamen procedatis. Contra vos universos et singulos et omnes alios qui sua crediderint interesse ad sedem apostolicam in hiis scriptis provocamus pro nobis et nobis adherentibus et etiam appellamus et apostolos instanter petimus nobis dari. Nos statum nostrum nostra et ecclesiarum predictarum bona protectioni sedis apostolice supponentes, et astantium et specialiter tabellionis publici hic presentis requirimus et sollicitamus memoriam que si opus fuerit in futurum nobis proficiat ad testimonium premissorum. Specialiter requirimus tabellionem hic presentem ut super premissis propositione protestatione oppositione contradictione et appellatione nobis faciat publicum instrumentum. Acta die martis post Remigium (*5 October 1294*) presentibus .. priore de Balneolis[205] Ambianensis diocesis, P. de Ona eius commonacho. Iidem decanus et capitulum predictam provocationem seu appellationem a procuratore suo una cum aliis procuratoribus cathedralium ecclesiarum Remensis provincie ut dictum est ad sedem apostolicam interiectam approbaverunt et ratificaverunt et pro ipsis et suo nomine factam esse voluerunt et etiam innovaverunt, ex habundanti prout dicta cedula continet ad sedem apostolicam provocantes seu appellantes ac predictam provocationem seu appellationem innovantes. Acta fuerunt hec in dicto capitulo sub anno die et indictione predictis, presentibus religioso viro fratre Milone canonico et preposito ecclesie Sancti Martini Laudunensis,[206] domino Radulpho rectore parochialis ecclesie de Grandiloco[207] Laudunensis diocesis, presbiteris Guillelmo de Grandiloco dicto de Porta et Johanne dicto Mouton de Foucoucourt dicte dyocesis clericis vocatis ad hoc testibus et rogatis.

(*Signum*) Ego Guillermus de Espri Bisuntine dyocesis clericus auctoritate sacrosancte Romane ecclesie publicus notarius premissis in dicto capitulo sic actis presens interfui et exinde hoc publicum instrumentum confectum signo meo consueto signavi et propria manu subscripsi rogatus.

3   **Petition from those having benefices and ecclesiastical goods in the dioceses of Thérouanne, Arras and Tournai presented, perhaps during this Council, to the archbishop and bishops of the province of Rheims.**
Printed here from the register of the abbey of Dunes: Bruges, Stadsbibliotheek MS 481, fo. 216r-v (item 364). It is printed also, from the same source, in Codex Dunensis, ed. KERVYN DE LETTENHOVE (see n. 29), no. 119. This petition appears (in the MS and not just in the printed edition) between documents concerning the assembly of Cistercian abbots and their grant of a subsidy to the king: see below K. There can be little doubt that it relates to the grant of biennial tenths to the king in 1294/5, and, since it refers to the grant as not yet having been made in the province of Rheims, it would seem to pre-date

---

[205]Bagneux (Somme, cant. de Doullens, com. de Gézaincourt).

[206]St Martin, Laon, Premonstratensian (Aisne, ch.-l. de dép.).

[207]Grandlup (Aisne, cant. de Marle, com. de Grandlup-et-Fay).

the making of the grant on 5 October. It seems likely, considering its provenance, that this letter relates especially to the ecclesiastical goods held by Cistercian abbeys (see K1, which follows it in the manuscript). Any consideration of the petition was perhaps considered unnecessary, or rendered ineffective, because of the separate assembly, probably already projected, of the Cistercian abbots, whose decisions were to concern the ecclesiastical goods of all Cistercian houses.

[R]everende pater et domine venerabilis Remensis archiepiscope, et vos reverendi patres domini episcopi eiusdem provincie, vobis supplicant habentes beneficia et bona ecclesiastica in Morinensi, Atrebatensi et Tornacensi dyocesibus quod, cum domini temporales dictarum dyocesium a personis predictis ecclesiasticis subventionem petierint et exigere inceperint et ab aliquibus iam receperint pro tuitione regni Francie contra Anglicos et alios inimicos versus illas partes, et non videatur equum quod pro eisdem causa et negotio subventionem bis solvant et ceteris beneficiatis in regno Francie plus graventur, quatenus laborare velitis cum effectu ut, si dicto domino regi subventionem facere contigerit, ab aliis dominis temporalibus liberentur, vel saltem portio quam forsan dictis dominis temporalibus solvent seu solverunt vel que ab eis exigentur, de subventione dicto regi facienda deducatur. Alias non est intentionis eorum ad subventionem aliquam faciendam domino regi se aliquatenus obligare. Item supplicant predicti quod omnes libertates et conditiones, que super dicta subventione ecclesiis cathedralibus conceduntur, eisdem pariter permittantur.

Appendix F.   COUNCIL OF THE PROVINCE OF NARBONNE AT BEZIERS, SHORTLY BEFORE 28 OCTOBER 1294

The date and place of this council are referred to in the grant of a subsidy by the exempt clergy of the province (see G2). The royal writ (below 1) is most unusual for it is an order to the bishop of Uzès, the little-known William de Gardies, to attend the council and to summon the clergy of his diocese to attend (see above pp. 15-16). It is claimed in Gallia Christiana that registers at Narbonne ('ex tabulis Narbonensibus') showed that the bishop of Uzès summoned the suffragans of the province to this council in the absence of the archbishop of Narbonne (Gilles Aycelin), acting either by ancient right because of the absence of the archbishop or as the archbishop's appointed vicar.[208] The evidence for this has not come to light. Archbishop Aycelin, active in royal service, could well have been absent from his province at the time that the summonses went out, though G2 tells us specifically that he was present at the council itself. The prelates and suffragan bishops also present are not named.

1   **Royal writ requiring the bishop of Uzès to attend the provincial council and to summon the clergy of his diocese**

Printed here from BN Lat. 11017, fo. 16r-v. Two copies from this source are in BN Languedoc 81, fos. 233r-v, 236r; and it is printed in MENARD (see n. 78), preuves p. 128 and, more accurately, in Claude DE VIC & Jean Joseph VAISSETE, Histoire générale de Languedoc, 16 vols, Toulouse, 1872-1905, 10, preuves pp. 302-3 (and calendared in MARTIN-CHABOT (see p. 38), no. 111).

---

[208]Gallia Christiana (see p. 46), 6, col. 632.

Philippus dei gratia Francorum rex dilecto et fideli nostro episcopo Uticensi salutem et dilectionem. Nuper in nostri tractatum extitit deliberatione consilii archiepiscopos, episcopos, prelatos, abbates, priores, prepositos, decanos, capitula, conventus, collegia tam cathedralium quam collegiatorum et conventualium, rectoresque ecclesiarum et ceteras personas ecclesiaticas regni nostri, propter quedam ardua negotia generalem statum regni eiusdem ac ecclesiarum et ecclesiasticarum personarum tangentia, que tractanda imminent hiis diebus, ad nostram presentiam convocare. Considerantes autem postmodum quod onerosum existeret et etiam sumptuosum singulos archiepiscopos, episcopos, abbates, priores, prepositos, decanos, capitula, conventus, collegia quam cathedralium quam collegiatorum et conventualium, rectoresque ecclesiarum et ceteras personas ecclesiasticas regni nostri in unum propter hoc convenire, ac volentes eis in hac parte consulere super laboribus et expensis, metropolitanorum etiam consideratione simili inductorum precibus annuentes, consilio deliberato providimus quod in unaquaque provincia metropolitanus episcopi prelati abbates priores prepositi decani capitula conventus collegia rectoresque ecclesiarum alieque persone predicte eiusdem provincie certis tempore et loco conveniant super huiusmodi negotiis tractaturi. Quapropter dilectionem vestram requirimus presentium tenore mandantes quatinus termino et loco quos dilectus et fidelis noster Narbonensis archiepiscopus metropolitanus vester vobis per suas litteras intimabit, ad tractandum conveniendum et ordinandum super hiis et ea quocumque modo tangentibus concordandum et firmandum eadem, prout conveniens et oportunum extiterit, personaliter intersitis, singulos abbates priores prepositos decanos capitula conventus collegia rectores ecclesiarum tam collegiatarum quam conventualium et parrochialium ceterasque personas vestre civitatis et diocesis non exemptas ex parte nostra requirentes attentius eisque per vestras litteras districte nichilominus iniungentes ut iidem abbates et priores conventuales ac prepositi personaliter, decani vero capitula conventus collegia rectores cetereque ecclesiastice persone per procuratores idoneos cum plenis et sufficientibus mandatis, ad tractandum ordinandum et conveniendum super hiis et ea ut premittitur contingentibus quovismodo ac concordandum et firmandum eadem, loco et termino compareant antedictis. Actum Parisius die martis post festum beati Petri ad vincula anno domini m^o cc^o lxxxx^o quarto. (*3 August 1294*)

Appendix G. ASSEMBLY OF THE EXEMPT CLERGY OF THE PROVINCE OF NARBONNE AT BEZIERS, 28-29 OCTOBER 1294

Summoned by the king for 28 October the assembly met in the king's palace at Béziers and granted a subsidy on 29 October. See above pp. 18-19.

1 **Royal summons to the assembly, following a letter and schedule concerning the summons from the king's clerk Peter de Mauloues**

Printed from BN Lat. 11017 fos. 21v-22v. Two copies from this source are in BN Languedoc 81, fos. 234r-v, 236r-v; and it is printed in MENARD (see n. 78), preuves pp. 128-9 (and calendared in MARTIN-CHABOT (see p. 38), nos. 122-3).

Anno domini m. cc. nonagesimo iiii^o die jovis post festum beati Mathei[209] apostoli (*23 September 1294*) recepit nobilis vir dominus Alfonsius de Rouvroyo, miles domini regis, senescallus Bellicadr', litteras quasdam venerabilis viri domini P[etri] de Mauloues, decani Sancti Quintini, clerici domini regis,[210] sigillo eius, ut prima facie apparebat, sigillatas, quibus erat anexa quedam cedula, quarum litterarum et cedule tenores sequuntur infrascripte:

P[etrus] de Mauloues, decanus Sancti Quintini, domini regis Francorum clericus, dilectis suis senescallis Tholose, Carcasson', et Bellicadri et Ruthene salutem et dilectionem. Significamus vobis quod dominus rex mittit ad vos per Stephanum de la Harnede, servientem suum in prepositura Parisius, literas suas exemptis provincie Narbonensis super quodam negotio ipsius domini regis mittendas, ut vos de eisdem faciatis prout in cedula presentibus hiis annexa continetur. Quare ex parte ipsius domini regis mandamus quatinus easdem a dicto Stephano recipiatis et de eisdem prout in dicta cedula continetur faciatis et ordinetis. Valete. Datum Parisius die jovis post decollationem beati Johannis Baptiste anno domini m^o cc^o nonagesimo iiii^o. (*2 September 1294*) Cedule vero tenor talis est: Le serians qui ira en la province de Narbon' ira au seneschal de Roergue & au seneschal de Tholose & au seneschal de Carcassone & a celui de Biauquaire, & monstrera a chaucun seneschal ou a son lieutenant la letre le roi & ceste cedule, & li seneschaus peurront la copie de la letre le roi sur leur seaus & lenvoieront a chaucun de leur ballis & prevoz ou de leur juges & leur manderont quil facent savoir a chaucun de leur prevoste ou de leur jugerie qui exemps est & qui demoure dedans la province de Narbone que il soit au jour & au lieu contenu dedanz la letre le roi, & que li abbe, li prevost, & le doien, & le prieur y soient en propres personnes, li convent & li chapitres par procurceur souffisanz, & soit la chose si diligaumenz faite que il ni ait nul deffauz. Et renvoieront li seneschaux par escrit les responses de ceus qui auront este aiorne au lieu la ou li concile sera & au ior a ceus qui la seront

---

[209]Mathie MS.

[210]See above n. 54.

envoi de par le roy & toutevois il sachent par les collecteurs du disieme des exemps le quil sont exempt, quar il ne le povent miex savoir que par ces collecteurs.

Item recepit dictus dominus senescallus litteras regias in hec verba: Philippus dei gratia Francorum rex dilectis et fidelibus nostris abbatibus prioribus prepositis decanis capitulis conventibus[211] collegiis ceterisque personis ecclesiasticis exemptis Narbonensis provincie ad quos presentes litere pervenerint salutem et dilectionem. Nuper in nostri tractatum extitit deliberatione consilii abbates priores prepositos decanos capitula conventus collegia ceterasque personas ecclesiasticas regni nostri exemptas et non exemptas, propter quedam ardua negotia generalem statum regni eiusdem ecclesiarum et ecclesiasticarum personarum tangentia que tractanda iminent hiis diebus, ad nostram presentiam convocare. Considerantes autem postmodum quod honerosum esset ac etiam sumptuosum singulos archiepiscopos episcopos abbates priores prepositos decanos capitula conventus et collegia tam cathedralium ecclesiarum et ceteras personas regni nostri exemptas et non exemptas in unum propter hoc convenire, ac volentes eis in hac parte consulere super laboribus et expensis, consilio deliberato providimus quod in unaquaque provincia abbates priores prepositi decani capitula conventus collegia alieque persone ecclesiastice eiusdem provincie exempte conveniant super huiusmodi negotio tracture. Vos itaque abbates priores prepositos decanos capitula conventus collegia ceterasque personas ecclesiasticas Narbonensis provincie exemptas, duximus requirendas quatinus, hac instanti die festi beatorum apostolorum Symonis et Jude (*28 October*) apud Bitterin convenire venerint ad tractandum et ordinandum super hiis confirmandum et firmandum eadem, in premissis taliter vos habentes quod nobis debeat esse gratum. Actum Parisius die mercurii post festum decollationis beati Johannis Baptiste anno domini m^o cc^o nonagesimo iiii^o. (*1 September 1294*)

2   Grant of biennial tenth
Printed from AN J712 no. 302/12.

Noverint universi et cetera ex parte domini regis Francie exempti provincie Narbonensis quantum in regno Francie se extendit citati apud Bitteris[212] diem iovis in festo apostolorum Simonis et Jude (*28 October*) anno domini m^o cc^o nonagesimo quarto ad tractandum ordinandum concordandum et firmandum cum gentibus domini regis super contentis in litteris regiis eisdem exemptis missis ipsa die iovis comparuerunt apud Bitteris coram venerabilibus viris dominis Geraldo de Malo Monte et Petro de Latiliacho

---

[211] collectoribus MS.

[212] The Latin name for Béziers appears in slightly different abbreviated forms in this document, which have been standardised to Biterris or the adjectival Biterrensis.

canonico Suesionense clericis domini regis ad Narbonensem provinciam per dominum regem destinatis pro negotio presenti, venerabiles patres infrascripti provincie Narbonensis personaliter, et procuratores quorundam absentium, videlicet (i) dominus Bertrandus abbas Electi[213] Narbonensis dyocesis pro se et suo conventu et suis officiariis, et nichilominus pro eodem conventu tanquam procurator seu sindicus frater Bernardus de Castro Porro monachus eiusdem monasterii, (ii) dominus Ramundus abbas sancti Pontii Thomeriarum[214] eiusdem diocesis pro se et suo conventu et suis officiariis, et nichilominus frater Fredolus monachus eiusdem monasterii pro eodem conventu tanquam procurator seu sindicus, (iii) dominus Sancius abbas monasterii Fontis Calidi[215] eiusdem diocesis pro se et suo conventu et suis officiariis, (iv) dominus Augerius abbas Crassen'[216] diocesis Carcassonensis pro se et suo conventu et suis officiariis et nichilominus pro suo conventu frater Berengarius Dalinasen helemosinarius procurator seu sindicus, (v) dominus Attrassacus abbas Jusselen'[217] Biterrensis diocesis pro se et eodem conventu et eius officiariis, et nichilominus frater Johannes Gambaudi monachus procurator seu sindicus eiusdem monasterii, (vi) dominus Ademarius abbas sancti Tiberii[218] Agacensis dyocesis pro se et suo conventu et suis officiariis, et nichilominus pro eodem conventu frater Guillelmus Genesii procurator seu sindicus, (vii) frater Ermandus prior de Pedenacio[219] monasterii Case dei[220] Agathensis dyocesis et de Portiano[221] Magalolensis dyocesis pro se et pro prioribus sancti Andree de Mesna,[222] Sancti Stephani de Lausacho[223] et Sancti Martini de Valasanicis[224] eiusdem eiusdem (sic) Agathensis dyocesis, (viii) frater Guillelmus Genesii prior Sancti Martini de Fenoloto[225] monasterii Sancti

---

[213]Alet (Aude, cant. de Limoux).

[214]St-Pons-de-Thomières (Hérault, cant.).

[215]Fontcaude (Premonstratensian) (Hérault, cant. de St-Chinian, com. de Cazedarnes).

[216]Lagrasse (Aude, cant.).

[217]Joncels (Hérault, cant. de Lunas).

[218]St-Thibéry (Hérault, cant. de Pézenas).

[219]Pézenas (Hérault, cant.).

[220]La Chaise-Dieu (Haute-Loire, cant. de Brioude).

[221]Poussan (Hérault, cant. de Mèze).

[222]Sesquiers (Hérault, cant. et com. de Mèze).

[223]Lieussac (Hérault, cant. et com. de Montagnac).

[224]St-Martin-de-Valleurargues (Hérault, cant. et com. de Pézenas).

[225]St-Martin-de-Fenouillet (Hérault, cant. de Pézenas, com. de St-Thibéry).

Tiberii[226] pro se, item pro priore Sancte Marie de Nataliano[227] eiusdem monasterii, (ix) dominus Guillelmus abbas sancti Guillelmi[228] Ludovensis dyocesis pro se et suo conventu et suis officiariis et nichilominus pro eodem conventu frater frater (sic) Johannes Gausberti monachus et procurator eiusdem conventus, (x) frater Johannes de Castaneto pro priore sancti Felicis de Leracio[229] et Sancti Petri de Fagia[230] monasterii Case dei, qui omnes predicti sunt de senescallia Carcassone, (xi) frater Bernardus de Ripperia canonicus monasterii Combe Longe[231] Coseranensis dyocesis ordinis Premostratenensis pro grangiis quas dictum monasterium habet tam in senescallia Carcassonense quam Tholosana, (xii) frater Ramundus de Sancto Iorio pro abbate et conventu de Capella[232] Tholosanensis dyocesis Premostratensis ordinis, (xiii) magister Johannes Vaschen' pro conventu et monasterio Sancti Saturnini Tholosane[233] procurator seu sindicus, qui est de senescallia Tholosana, (xiv) dominus Ramundus abbas Sancti Egidii[234] Nemausensis dyocesis pro se et suo conventu et suis officiariis et nichilominus frater Hugo de Falequerio prior maior claustralis eiusdem canventus pro ipso conventu procurator seu sindicus, (xv) dominus Petrus abbas Salmpmoden'[235] eiusdem diocesis pro se et suo conventu et suis officiariis, (xvi) frater Bermundus prior de Barsacho[236] monasterii Case dei pro se et pro priore Sancti Boudilii prope Nemausum,[237] item pro prioribus de Aguileriis[238] de Auseto[239] de Boqueto[240] et de

---

[226]St-Thibéry (Hérault, cant. de Pézenas).

[227]Nadailhan (Hérault, cant. de Pézenas, com. de St-Thibéry).

[228]St-Guilhem-le-Désert (Hérault, cant. d'Aniane).

[229]St-Félix-de-l'Héras (Hérault, cant. du Caylar).

[230]St-Pierre-de-la-Fage (Hérault, cant. de Lodève).

[231]Combelongue (in dioc. of Couserans, prov. of Auch) (Ariège, cant. de St-Girons, com. de Rimont).

[232]La Capelette (Haute-Garonne, cant. de Grenade, com. de Merville).

[233]St-Sernin, Toulouse (Haute-Garonne, ch.-l. de dép.).

[234]St-Gilles (Gard, cant.).

[235]Psalmody (Gard, cant. et com. de St-Gilles).

[236]Bizac (Gard, cant. de Sommières, com. de Calvisson).

[237]St-Baudile (Gard, cant. et com. de Nîmes).

[238]Argilliers (Gard, cant. de Remoulins).

[239]Scribal error for 'Broseto': Brouzet-lès-Alès (Gard, cant. de Vézenobres).

[240]Bouquet (Gard, cant. de St-Ambroix).

Planis[241] Uticensis dyocesis, (xvii) frater Bertrandus de Garda Marsiliensis monachus prior de Blannavis[242] Uticensis dyocesis, (xviii) frater Amedeus prior Bonorum Vallium[243] Uticensis dyocesis ordinis Sancti Ruffi pro se, item pro prioribus de Aujacho[244] et Sancti Andree de Crugeria[245] eiusdem ordinis et eiusdem dyocesis, (xix) Guillelmus de Vilareto procurator prioris de Arreis[246] monasterii Marsiliensis dyocesis Nemausensis et priorum de Vicano[247] et de Alsona[248] eiusdem monasterii et eiusdem dyocesis senescallie Bellicadri, omnes die veneris in crastinum dicti festi coram prenominatis dominis clericis domini regis in palatio Biterrensi domini regis comparentes unanimiter et concorditer deliberato consilio requisitione eis facta per dictos dominos clericos domini regis super dicta subventione domino regi facienda et expositis eis causis et rationibus prout decuit obtulerunt sponte et gratiose et sua bona et mera liberalitate eisdem dominis Geraldo et Petro clericis domini regis pro ipso domino rege recipientibus decimam suorum reddituum seu proventuum eorum que habent in regno Francie ad tempus et modis et formis et conditionibus quibus prelati et alii ordinarii eiusdem provincie Narbonensis in concilio Biterrensi per dominum archiepiscopum Narbonensem cum suis suffraganeis pridie celebrato concesserunt domino regi salvo quod solutio per eos exemptos [neque] ordinariis neque ordinariorum collectoribus fiat set collectores eis de suo ordine deputentur et collectoribus quos de suo ordine dominus rex deputaverit specialibus exsolvenda. Acta firmiter hec in palatio Biterrensi domini regis anno et die veneris quibus supra (*29 October*) in presentia et testimonio domini Petri Radimundi iudicis maioris domini senescalli Carcassonensis et Biterrensis, domini Sicardi de Nauro iudicis maioris in senescallia Tholosana, Johannis de Inucta receptoris domini regis reddituum suorum in senescallia Carcassonensi et Biterrensi, magistri Petri Melen de Castris notarii curie appellationum Tholosane, et plurium aliorum et mei Arnaudi Basini notarii curie Carcassone domini regis qui predictis presens interfui et requisitus hanc cartam recepi acque scripsi et signo meo signavi regnante serenissimo domino Philippo rege Francie.

---

[241] Les Plans (Gard, cant. d'Alès-est).

[242] Blannaves (Gard, cant. de La Grand-Combe, com. de Branoux).

[243] Bonnevaux (Gard, cant. de Génolhac).

[244] Aujac (Gard, cant. de Génolhac).

[245] St-André-de-Cruzières (Ardèche, cant. des Vans).

[246] Arre (Gard, cant. du Vigan).

[247] Le Vigan (Gard, ch.-l. d'arr.).

[248] Alzon (Gard, cant.).

Appendix H.   COUNCIL OF THE PROVINCE OF BORDEAUX AT PONS, AUTUMN 1294
Entries in Robert Mignon's inventory of royal accounts indicate that an ecclesiastical council met at Pons in the diocese of Saintes. Since the biennial tenth granted there was raised between the feast of All Saints 1294 and the feast of All Saints 1296, it seems that the council met in the autumn of 1294; and since the entries show that accounts were presented for tenths collected in the province of Bordeaux, and not simply the diocese of Saintes, it appears that the council at Pons was a provincial council. The third of the entries printed below suggests that accounts may have been presented specifically from the dioceses of Bordeaux ('Burdegalensis'), Périgueux ('Petragoricensis') and Agen ('Agennensis'). It is most unlikely that money was collected only from these dioceses, but further entries in the inventory (see no. 754 and the first part of no. 752) referring to the other three dioceses of the province (Angoulême, Poitiers and Saintes) relate apparently to the later tenths granted to the king in 1297 and 1298.[249]

1   **Inventory of accounts**
The following items are taken from Inventaire, ed. LANGLOIS (see n. 18), nos. 701, 705, 752 (edited from BN Lat. 9069).

a) Decima biennalis seu subventio per modum decime a prelatis sua propria auctoritate regi Philippo Pulchro in concilio apud Pontem, Xanctonensis diocesis, celebrato anno $m^o cc^o iiii^{xx} xiv^o$ concessa pro subsidio regni, levata ab Omnibus Sanctis tunc usque ad idem festum $m^o cc^o iiii^{xx} xvi^o$, per biennium....
b) Alius compotus eorundem[250] de eadem decima pro duobus terminis primi anni, videlicet $m^i cc^j iiii^{xx} xiv^j$, in provinciis Turonensi et Burdegalensi, factus per Johannem de Placentia vigesima secunda Martii $m^o cc^o iiii^{xx} xvi^o$. Corrigitur finis, et pauca signantur esse corrigenda.
c) Compotus magistri Symonis Festu, decani Blesensis ... de eisdem duplicibus decimis[251] ac de decima biennali anni $m^i cc^j iiii^{xx} xiv^j$ in diocesibus Vasatensi, Burdegalensi et Lemovicensi, Petragoricensi, Caturcensi, Tholosana, Agennensi, Auxitanensi, Coseranensi, Convenarum, Tarviensi, Lectorensi, Adurensi, Olerensi, Ascurensi et Acquensi,[252] factus jovis post Epiphaniam $m^o cc^o iiii^{xx} xix^o$. Plura videntur per eum esse recuperanda.

---

[249] See Strayer, 'Consent to taxation', pp. 30-2.

[250] i.e. Bichii et Moucheti.

[251] i.e. the double tenths granted in 1297 and 1298.

[252] i.e. the dioceses of Bazas (prov. of Auch), Bordeaux, Limoges (prov. of Bourges), Périgueux (prov. of Bordeaux), Cahors (prov. of Bourges), Toulouse (prov. of Narbonne), Agen (prov. of Bordeaux), and Auch, Couserans, Comminges, Tarbes, Lectoure, Aire-sur-l'Adour, Oloron, Lescar and Dax (all in the prov. of Auch).

Appendix I.   ASSEMBLY OF PREMONSTRATENSIAN ABBOTS AT ST-QUENTIN, ON OR SHORTLY BEFORE 9 FEBRUARY 1295

The grant of a subsidy below in a letter from the abbot of Prémontré provides the only evidence for this assembly of the abbots of the order in France.

1   Grant of biennial tenth

Printed here from original in AN J1035 no. 37: 23cm. X 35cm. + 1cm. (pli); in the bottom right-hand corner 'Th. (*or* Ch.) Gueroudi';[253] supra pli 'collatio facta est per ?R. de Perer"; slit for one seal tag; on dorse in contemporary hand 'copia littere cum concessione decime Premonstraten".

Universis presentes litteras inspecturis .. officialis curie Parisiensis salutem in domino. Noveritis nos anno domini m^o cc^o nonagesimo quarto die veneris ante brandones (*18 February 1295*) litteras inferius annotatas vidisse in hec verba. Universis presentes litteras visuris G[uillelmus][254] dei patientia Premonstratensis abbas salutem in domino. Ad puplicam mondi notitiam a pricis (*sic*) temporibus iam pervenit quod benedictum regnum Francie pre ceteris mondi regnis hactenus extitit orthodoxe fidei munimentum et invincibile presidium catholice puritatis in quo semper pax viguit fides crevit catholica et religio Christiana auctore domino suscepit felicia incrementa. Nam sub protectione pacifici principis domini regis nostri suorumque progenitorum regum Francie amotis offendiculis gallicana fuit ecclesia in pacis pulcritudine et requie opulenta et illa mutua caritate que inter personas ecclesiasticas principes et barones dicti regni Francie concurrebat fruemur imposterum domino permittente. Attendentes igitur quod rex Anglie ex concepta diu nequitia, ut rumor moscus enuntiat, confederatus cum quibusdam magnis et potentibus extra regnum, quos ad hoc muneribus et aliis diversis machinationibus callide sibi noscitur induxisse, sicut evidenter apparet, aspiret ad turbationem pacis in eodem regno et ad impugnationem hostillem regis regnique sui suadente diabolo, qui semper satagit inter fratres discordiam seminare, prout eiusdem regis Anglie excessus notorii manifesta facinora et execrabilia cognamina multipliciter detestantur, et quia iacula que previdentur minus feriunt atque ledunt, vias exquirimus ut idem rex noster et dominus regnumque suum et cohabitantes in eo ab impugnationibus hostium securius valeat se tueri, si forte regem aut regnum seu partem ipsius impugnari, quod absit, hostiliter contingeret quoquomodo, nuper in convocatione abbatum nostri ordinis regni Francie apud Sanctum Quintinum in Viromandua propter hoc specialiter per nos facta diligenti deliberatione prehabita providimus (i) fore subveniendum domino nostro regi ad nostram et eiusdem regni deffensionem, prout evidens neccessitas id exposcit, partem decimam omnium redituum et proventuum ecclesiarum nostri ordinis in

---

[253]The notary commonly added his name in this way: see Paul FOURNIER, Les officialités au moyen age, Paris, 1880, pp. 302-3.

[254]Guillelmus de Louvignies (see Gallia Christiana (above p. 46), 11, col. 652).

regno Francie existentium propter dictam neccessitatem verisimiliter iminentem de consensu unanimi et concordi nostro et omnium tunc inibi personaliter existentium necnon procuratorum personarum absentium, sub certa forma quam sedes apostolica hactenus observavit, dicto domino regi hac vice per biennium de speciali gratia concedentes quod per Sancti Martini Laudunensis[255] et Cuissiacensis[256] abbates nostri ordinis quos ad hoc deputavimus fideliter apud Laudunum in infrascriptis terminis colligetur. (ii) Ita quod medietatem ipsius infra instantem quindenam Pasche (*17 April 1295*) et aliam medietatem infra quindenam nativitatis beati Johannis baptiste postea subsequentis (*8 July 1295*) et eisdem loco et terminis anni immediate sequentis predictis receptoribus quilibet modo quo supra solvere teneatur prefatis abbatibus et procuratoribus in hoc consentientibus penitus et expresse. (iii) Et si forte aliqui in predictis terminis ipsam decimam partem solvere distulerint, ad id per censuram ecclesiasticam et aliter compellentur, nec regales ad hoc se ullatenus intromittent, nisi a receptoribus super hoc deputatis specialiter fuerint evocati. (iv) Iidemque receptores pecuniam quam exinde exegerint et receperint in hac parte assignabunt in Lauduno domino regi vel illi aut illis quibus idem dominus rex eam ordinaverit exhiberi. (v) Ita tamen quod si durante dicto biennio decimam seu maius onus aut simile in eodem regno per sedem apostolicam concedi vel imponi contigerit vel iam etiam sit concessum seu (vi) domino inspirante cui non est difficile disiuncta coniungere pax inter dictos reges durante dicto biennio reformetur ex toto cessabitur a solutione partis decime supradicte. (vii) Si vero dicto tempore treugam inter eosdem reges iniri contigerit quod illo tempore quo treuga duraverit antedicta huiusmodi solutio totaliter suspendetur. In cuius rei testimonium presentes litteras fieri fecimus et sigilli nostri munimine roborari. Datum et actum apud Sanctum Quintinum in Viromandua anno domini m^o cc^o nonagesimo quarto in octabis purificationis beate Marie virginis. (*9 February 1295*) Transcriptum autem huiusmodi litterarum fieri fecimus sub sigillo curie Parisiensis salvo iure cuiuslibet anno et die veneris predictis.

---

[255]St Martin, Laon (Aisne, ch.-l. de dép.).

[256]Cuissy-et-Geny (Aisne, cant. de Craonne).

Appendix J.   COUNCIL OF THE PROVINCE OF LYONS AT MACON, 9 FEBRUARY 1295
The date of the council is provided by the grant below. The council was presided over by the
suffragan bishop of Autun, Hugh d'Arcy, administrator of the archbishopric of Lyons *sede
vacante* (Berald de Got had been made cardinal bishop of Albano by Celestine V in September
1294).[257] Several abbots were present, as well as the bishop of Chalon-sur-Saône, proctors
of the cathedral chapter of Langres *sede vacante* and the official of the bishop of Mâcon *in
remotis agentis.*

1   **Grant of biennial tenth**
Printed here from original in AN J1035 no. 36: 35cm. X 29cm. + 4cm. (pli); slits for 12
seal tags, remnants of five seals; on dorse in contemporary hand 'super concessione decime
Lugdunensis provincie, xix'.

Universis presentes litteras inspecturis miseratione divina Hugo Eduensis
gerens administrationem archiepiscopatus Lugdunensis ipsius sede vacante,
Guillelmus Cabilonensis episcopi, Petrus archidiaconus et Johannes de
Pleopapa canonicus Lingonensis procuratores capituli Lingonensis sede
vacante, et Hugo de Kadrellis officialis Maciscononsis gerens vices domini
Nicolai dei gratia episcopi nunc in remotis agentis suffraganei ecclesie
Lugdunensis salutem in domino. Ad publicam mundi notitiam a priscis
temporibus iam pervenit quod benedictum regnum Francie pre ceteris mundi
regnis fuit orthodoxe fidei munimentum et invincibile presidium catholice
puritatis in quo semper pax viguit fides crevit catholica et religio Christiana
auctore domino suscepit felicia incrementa. Attendentes igitur quod rex
Anglie ex concepta diu nequitia quibusdam magnis et potentibus extra
regnum confederatis sibi, quos ad hoc muneribus et aliis diversis
machinationibus callide dicitur induxisse, aspiret ad turbationem pacis dicti
regni et ad impugnationem hostilem regis regnique sui diabolo suadente, qui
semper satagit inter fratres discordiam seminare, prout eiusdem regis Anglie
excessus notorii manifesta facinora multipliciter detestantur et fama publica
predicat et testatur, quia vero iacula que previdentur minus feriunt atque
ledunt, vias exquirimus per quas idem rex noster et dominus regnumque
suum et cohabitantes in eo ab impugnationibus hostium securius valeat se
tueri si regem aut regnum seu partem ipsius, quod absit, impugnari hostiliter
contingeret quoquomodo, nuper in convocatione provinciali propter hoc
specialiter apud Matisconem per nos facta episcopum Eduensem diligenti
deliberatione prehabita de consensu unanimi et concordi nostro et omnium
tunc inibi existentium necnon procuratorum personarum absentium
subveniendum fore providimus (i) domino nostro regi ad nostram et
ecclesiarum nostrarum ac eiusdem regni defensionem prout necessitas
evidens id exposcit sub forma que sequitur videlicet quod per biennium
tantum levetur nomine subventionis domino regi Francie faciende de bonis

---

[257]EUBEL (see n. 80), 1, p. 11 and Jean-Baptiste MARTIN, Conciles et bullaire du diocèse
de Lyon, Lyons, 1905, p. 501.

ecclesiasticis quantum solebat levari et exigi a quolibet beneficiato pro subsidio terre sancte et ab illis tantum a quibus decima exigebatur secundum declarationem et taxationem antiquam factam pro dicto subsidio terre sancte, conditionibus infrascriptis: (ii) Primo quod idem dominus rex precipiat si placet ut iniurias et gravamina per gentes suas ecclesiis et ecclesiasticis personis illata faciat revocari. (iii) Item, si pax fiat dicta subventio omnino tollatur. (iv) Item, si treuga fiat dicta subventio ipsa treuga durante suspendatur. (v) Item, si dominus papa decimam ipsi regi vel alii concesserit vel iam concessit vel aliud onus imposuerit ipsis personis ecclesiasticis omnino cesset subventio supradicta. (vi) Item, quod dicta subventio non levetur per gentes regis sed per unum canonicum ecclesie cathedralis et per alium quem elegerit quilibet episcopus in sua diocese vel capitulum ipsius ecclesie sede vacante. (vii) Item, quod si rex permittat quod duces comites seu barones petant vel exigant ab aliquibus de predictis personis subsidium alias non debitum, cessabit subventio memorata quantum ad illas personas vel rex faciet cessare personas antedictas. (viii) Item, quod si rex predicta omnia et singula acceptaverit sub modo et forma predictis suas patentes litteras dabit de predictis conventionibus firmiter observandis (ix) et quod nullum preiudicium dictis personis ecclesiasticis et ecclesiis suis propter hoc generetur nec ius aliquod ipsi regi vel eius successoribus imposterum acquiratur. (x) Item, quod nichil exigatur a personis vel rebus extra regnum Francie existentibus. (xi) Item, quod dicta subventio duobus terminis anno quolibet dictorum duorum annorum persolvatur et prima solutio fiat in festo nativitatis domini quod erit anno domini millesimo ducentesimo nonagesimo quinto (*25 December 1295*), secunda vero in festo nativitatis beati Johannis baptiste immediate sequenti (*24 June 1296*) pro primo anno, pro secundo autem in terminis supradictis. In cuius rei testimonium sigilla nostra una cum sigillis religiosorum virorum .. sancti Martini Eduensis[258] .. sancti Leonardi de Corbuneyo[259] .. Umgiaci[260] et sancte Margarete[261] Eduensis diocesis .. sancti Benigni Divionensis[262] .. sancti Secani[263] .. beate Marie de Castellione[264] Lingonensis diocesis monasteriorum abbatum in dicta convocatione personaliter existentium duximus presentibus apponenda. Datum Matisconem anno domini millesimo ducentesimo

---

[258]St-Martin, Autun (Saône-et-Loire, ch.-l. d'arr.).

[259]Corbigny (Nièvre, cant.).

[260]Oigny (Côte-d'Or, cant. de Baigneux-les-Juifs).

[261]Ste-Marguerite (Côte-d'Or, cant. de Beaune-nord, com. de Bouilland).

[262]St-Bénigne, Dijon (Côte-d'Or, ch.-l. de dép.).

[263]Saint-Seine-l'Abbaye (Côte-d'Or, cant.).

[264]Châtillon-sur-Seine (Côte-d'Or, cant.).

nonagesimo quarto die mercurii in octavis purificationis virginis gloriose. (*9 February 1295*)

Appendix K. ASSEMBLY OF THE CISTERCIAN ABBOTS OF CITEAUX, LA FERTE, PONTIGNY, CLAIRVAUX AND MORIMOND AT DIJON AFTER 5 OCTOBER 1294 AND BEFORE 3 APRIL 1295

The first document printed here was from the Cistercian abbeys of Dunes and Ter-Doest, and perhaps others holding ecclesiastical goods in the dioceses of Thérouanne, Arras and Tournai (see E3 above, which precedes it in the manuscript). It must pre-date the assembly of abbots, for there is no indication in the text that the decision concerning the subsidy to the king from the two abbeys would in fact be taken by the abbots of the Cistercian order rather than by the archbishop and bishops of the province. Since it refers to the provincial council at Compiègne (held on 5 October 1294) as having recently met, we can infer that the assembly of abbots took place later. The *terminus ad quem* is provided by 2 which refers to the first term of the grant. From the reference to the presence of Robert of Cîteaux in 2 we may infer an early rather than a late date, for Robert had been made a cardinal on 18 September; but he had not, it seems, reached the papal curia by the time of Celestine V's resignation in December.[265]

1   **Request from the abbeys of Dunes and Ter-Doest, addressed it seems to the archbishop of Rheims, that steps be taken to ensure that they do not pay subsidies to both the king of France and the count of Flanders**
Printed here from the register of the abbey of Dunes: Bruges, Stadsbibliotheek MS 481, fos 216v-217r (item 365). It is printed also, from the same source, in Codex Dunensis, ed. KERVYN DE LETTENHOVE (see n. 29), no. 120.

[C]um illustris comes talis pro tuitione terre sue subventionem sibi in certis et taxatis summis non modicis etiam per saisinam bonorum nostrorum exhiberi iam postulaverit cum effectu, et nichilominus in concilio Compendiensi nuper habito Francorum regi a prelatis et personis ecclesiasticis, sicut intelleximus, in Remensi provincia decima[266] sit concessa, grave quoque foret, nec equum videretur quod utrique domino de eisdem bonis ac pro eodem negotio solveremus, dilectioni vestre benigne mandamus quatenus peritos nostri ordinis consulatis et an primi abbates subventionem huiusmodi decime secundum formam datam in predicto concilio Compendiensi promiserint seu compositionem aliquam inierint pro certa pecunie quantitate, et quia alias in huiusmodi compositionibus [et] taxationibus fuimus non modicum pregravati de bonis nostris solvendo, tanquam omnia in regno Francie extitissent, presertim cum nos de Dunis maiorem partem bonorum nostrorum et nos de Capella ultra duas partes sub Imperio habeamus, et onus subventionis seu decime huiusmodi sit reale, cure vestre sit huiusmodi gravamen predictis patribus reverendis et aliis

---

[265]HERDE (see n. 79), p. 100.

[266]decima *interlined*.

quibuscunque necesse fuerit proponere et ostendere cum diligentia et effectu, et quid inde factum fuerit seu consultum rescribatis, intimantes quod quicquid pro subventione domini regis nobis impositum fuerit de bonis nostris extra regnum Francie solvendi domino comiti necessitas imminebit.

2 Grant of a biennial tenth, within an acceptance by the king
Printed here from the register of the abbey of Dunes: Bruges, Stadsbibliotheek MS 481, fos 215r-216r (item 363). It is printed also, from the same source, in Codex Dunensis, ed. KERVYN DE LETTENHOVE (see n. 29), no. 118 and, in abbreviated form and less accurately, in KERVYN DE LETTENHOVE, Etudes (see n. 29), cols. 1838-9.

[P]hilippus dei gratia Francorum rex notum facimus universis quod cum Cisterciensis de Firmitate de Pontiniaco de Claravalle et de Morimundo monasteriorum abbates pro se ac personis aliis monasteriorum et locorum aliorum Cisterciensis ordinis regni nostri decimam suorum ecclesiasticorum proventuum nobis ad biennium integrum in subsidium pro defensione et felici statu regni nostri sub certis modis et conditionibus duxerint liberaliter concedendam, prout in eorum litteris inde confectis plenius continetur, quarum tenor talis est: Excellentissimo principi domino suo Philippo dei gratia Francorum regi illustrissimo devoti eius fratres Robertus de Cistercio, Rufinus de Firmitate, Symon de Pontiniaco, Johannes de Claravalle et Dominicus de Morimundo monasteriorum abbates Cisterciensis ordinis, Cabilonensis Autissiodorensis et Lingonensis dyocesium eorumque monasteriorum conventus cum incrementis pacis et concordie successus prosperos ac felices. Ad publicam mundi notitiam a priscis temporibus iam pervenit quod benedictum regnum Francorum pre ceteris mundi regnis hactenus extitit orthodoxe fidei munimentum et invincibile presidium catholice puritatis in quo quidem regno vestro semper pax viguit fides crevit catholica et religio Christiana auctore domino suscepit felicia incrementa, et exulata extra regni vestri terminos discordia, que palmites suos tetendit usque ad maris terminos, suscipiet in futurum, ad cuius extirpationem sive exilium necessarium fore credimus subsidium omnium, quibus dicti regni vestri tranquillitas maxime pacem reddat statum parum tranquillum ac securum. Hinc est quod nos abbates predicti, regni vestri pacem et tranquillitatem affectantes, apud Divionem propter hoc specialiter congregati, diligenti deliberatione prehabita, providimus (i) a nobis et ab omnibus monachorum monasteriis nobis subiectis, dumtaxat in dicto regno vestro existentibus, fore subveniendum vobis ad dicte discordie exulationem, prout necessitas evidens id exposcit, partem decimam omnium reddituum et proventuum omnium monasteriorum monachorum[267] nostri ordinis in regno vestro existentium, propter dictam necessitatem, reddituumque et proventuum dumtaxat que dicta monasteria in vestro regno percipiunt et

[267]monachorum *interlined*.

consueverunt percipere et habere, et que ab ipsis monasteriis percipi contigerit et haberi, sub certa tamen forma quam sedes apostolia hactenus observavit, vobis hac vice per biennium et nomine nostri ordinis Cisterciensis de speciali gratia concedentes. (ii) Que quidem pars decima per unumquemque nostrum sive successores nostros, in generatione cuiuslibet in regno vestro existente, infrascriptis terminis in conscientiis nostris ac subditorum nostrorum absque dolo vel fraude fideliter colligetur. (iii) Cui fidei nostre stabitur absque alia retractatione penitus et expresse, ita quod medietatem ipsius in instanti resurrectione domini (*3 April 1295*), et aliam medietatem in festo omnium sanctorum proximo subsequente (*1 November 1295*), et eisdem terminis anni immediate sequentis quilibet abbas et conventus monasteriorum predictorum cuilibet nostrum seu successoribus nostris, prout cuiuslibet generatio distinguitur, modo quo supra solvere teneantur. (iv) Quam nobis solutam aut successoribus nostris a subditis nostris predictis, cum portione quemlibet nostrum aut successores nostros contingente, prout supradictum est, vobis vel certo mandato vestro tenebimur assignare. Et si forte aliqui in predictis terminis non ipsam partem decimam solvere distulerint, ad id per censuram nostri ordinis vel aliter compellentur. Nec vos, domine rex, per vos vel per alium de hoc aliquem compelletis, nisi a nobis aut nostrum altero super hoc specialiter fueritis evocatus, (v) et si forte, durante dicto biennio, decimam seu majus onus aut simile in vestro regno per sedem apostolicam concedi vel imponi contigerit vel iam etiam sit concessum, (vi) seu, domino inspirante, cui non est difficile disiuncta coniungere, pax regno vestro benedicto reddita fuerit, ex toto cessabitur a solutione partis decime supradicte. (vii) Si vero dicto tempore treugam super dicta discordia iniri contigerit, pro illo tempore quo treuga duraverit, antedicta huiusmodi solutio totaliter suspendetur, (viii) ita tamen quod propter solutionem huiusmodi vos dicere non possitis, nec debeatis vobis ius acquisitum esse in futurum super subventionibus et subsidiis similibus aut aliis faciendis vobis aut concedendis a nobis aut nostris, quod per presentes non intendimus concedere ullo modo. In cuius rei testimonium presentibus litteris sigilla nostra duximus apponenda. Datum etc. Nos huiusmodi decimale subsidium sic oblatum sub modis et conditionibus antedictis tenore presentium acceptamus, modos et conventiones easdem approbantes expresse. In cuius rei testimonium presentibus litteris nostrum fecimus sigillum apponi. Datum etc.

3   **Letters from the abbot of Cîteaux announcing the decision to pay a subsidy and warning the other abbots of the Order not to pay a subsidy to anyone else**
Printed here from the register of the abbey of Dunes: Bruges, Stadsbibliotheek MS 481, fos 217r-218r (items 367 & 366). The letters are printed also, from the same source, in Codex Dunensis, ed. KERVYN DE LETTENHOVE (see n. 29), nos. 122 & 121. The first part of a), as far as 'duximus ordinandum quod', is printed also, but less accurately, in KERVYN DE LETTENHOVE, Etudes (see n. 29), col. 1839.

a) Salutem[268] et cum sincera in domino caritate patientiam in adversis. Cum nuper ex parte excellentissimi principis dei gratia Francorum regis de Cisterciensi et ceterorum monasteriorum abbatibus nomine totius ordinis lamentose fuerit expositum benedictum regnum Francie inimicorum graves sustinere molestias et incursus, propter quos omnium nostrum et subditorum nostrorum tranquillitas impugnatur, nobisque et nostris monasteriis minatur periculum ac ruinam, nisi dictis molestiis et incursibus occurratur, ad que dicti regni vires parum sufficiunt, propter quod predictis abbatibus et nobis fecit humiliter supplicari quod nos auxilium et consilium eidem adhibere curaremus ad extirpandas dictas molestias et incursus, quatenus exulatis dictis molestiis et periculis nos et subditi nostri pacis testamento sicuti hactenus freti fuimus frueremur, nos vero, attendentes dicta pericula imminere nobis et vobis et generaliter omnibus dicti regni, attendentes insuper per iactum mercium dicti regis quas[269] quidem merces necesse habet exponere propter pericula supradicta nostras salvas existere et personas, propter que secundum naturalis equitatis rationem et sanctiones legitimas debemus de bonis nobis a deo collatis ad supportandum tante molis pondus subvenire. Quocirca supradicti abbates et nos apud Divionem propter hoc specialiter congregati, nomine cuiuslibet nostrum et totius ordinis, de bonorum consilio duximus ordinandum quod pars decima omnium reddituum et proventuum omnium monasteriorum monachorum nostri ordinis in dicto regno Francie existentium, proventuum inquam et reddituum dumtaxat que dicta monasteria in dicto regno percipiunt et consueverunt percipere et habere, per tempus biennii colligatur, et in duobus terminis, videlicet in resurrectione domini (*3 April 1295*) et in festo beati Remigii subsequente (*1 October 1295*), patri abbati assignetur, ubi dictus pater duxerit assignandum. Estimatio vero seu collatio dictorum proventuum et reddituum conscientiis abbatum et suorum subditorum relinquetur, quam estimationem sepedictam abbates et nos bona fide et sine fraude in conscientiis nostris et subditorum nostrorum dicto regi promisimus, prout in quadam littera eidem tradita et ab eodem accepta, quam secum defert lator presentium, plenius videbitis contineri. Hinc est quod nos auctoritate abbatum predictorum et nostra, in virtute sancte obedientie et sub pena excommunicationis, vobis damus firmiter in mandatis quatenus vos et vestrum quilibet dictam partem decimam de dictis proventibus et redditibus monateriorum vestrorum in conscientiis vestris et subditorum vestrorum secundum modum et formam quibus supra colligatis, et medietatem dicte partis decime in resurrectione

---

[268]The text as printed in KERVYN DE LETTENHOVE, Etudes, col. 1839, begins 'Venerabilibus et in Christo karissimis coabbatibus salutem...'. Although this is incorrect, the content of the letter suggests that it was indeed addressed to the co-abbots of the Order, like b) below which precedes it in the MS.

[269]necesse habet *crossed through.*

domini (*3 April 1295*), et aliam medietatem in festo omnium sanctorum proximo subsequente (*1 November 1295*) nobis apud Parisius assignetis, et sic anno secundo biennii totidem, loco et terminis antedictis, et filiis vestris in dicto regno pro toto vel pro parte dictorum proventuum existentibus detis in mandatis, auctoritate modo et forma quibus nostrum mandatum recipitis, ut partem dicte decime colligere et nobis assignare non omittant, prout superius est expressum, scientes quod si[270] in premissis inobedientes extiteritis vel fraudem aliquam feceritis, si propter huiusmodi defectum seu fraudem nos vel vos a regalibus contigerit in aliquo molestari, nos qui in hac parte sumus pro vobis obligati et defensionis clipeus constituti, si necesse fuerit, bona vestra pro quanto defeceritis eisdem regalibus exponemus, et ne super huiusmodi mandati nostri receptione in aliquo tueri possitis, vobis universis et singulis districtissime precipimus ut una cum sigillo nostro sigilla vestra, vel priores vestri si vos abbates contigerit abesse, presentibus quandocumque vobis presentate fuerint apponatis. Datum etc.

b) [V]enerabilibus et in Christo karissimis coabbatibus eius et eorum conventibus ad quos presentes littere pervenerint, talis salutem et in agendis constantiam salutarem. Cum per[271] nos illustrissimo principi dei gratia Francorum regi specialiter concessum sit ut omnia monasteria nostri ordinis in suo regno existentia, de omnibus proventibus et redditibus quos per hoc instans biennium percipient, decimam partem in subsidium eiusdem regni assignent integraliter absque fraude, propter guerrarum molestias que hiis diebus imminent dicto regno, domino permittente, ne propter hoc vos aut vestrum aliquos contingat, quod absit, duplici taxatione conteri circa negotium huiusmodi vos premonitos esse volumus, vobis omnibus et singulis benigne mandantes quatenus, si occasione guerrarum huiusmodi ab aliis quibuscunque dominis ducibus comitibus vicecomitibus baronibus militibus seu aliis quibuscunque vos vel vestrum aliquem contigerit impeti vel exactione qualibet molestari, eiusdem domini regis protectione et auxilio vos et bona vestra secundum tenorem littere ipsius domini regis, cuius transcriptum presenti cedule inseri fecimus, defendatis.

---

[270] si *interlined.*

[271] per *interlined.*

4   **Royal order to the seneschal of Beaucaire to refrain from any further actions against the Cistercians since a subsidy has been granted**
Printed here from BN Lat. 11017, fo. 76v. It is printed also in MARTIN-CHABOT (see p. 38), p. 162, no. 257.

Philippus etc senescallo nostro Belliquadri vel eius locum tenenti salutem. Cum dilecti et fideles nostri abbas Cysterciensis ceterique abbates eiusdem ordinis in regno nostro pro se et eorum conventibus ad defencionem regni nostri predicti subsidium gratum nobis fecerint et acceptum, mandamus vobis quatinus bona omnia et singula predictorum abbatum et ordinis, si que de mandato nostro in vestra senescallia vel eius resorto fuerint arrestata, dearrestetis visis presentibus seu dearrestari penitus faciatis, garnisiones etiam saisinas et impedimenta quecumque a bonis et domibus ipsorum amoveatis seu faciatis absque dilatione qualibet amoveri, dampna quoque, si que nostra occasione incurrerint vel eis a quoquam collata fuerint, faciatis eisdem restitui et etiam restaurari, nichil, ratione novitatis cuiuslibet vel statuti hactenus minime consueti, petentes seu exigentes aut peti vel exigi permittentes ab ipsis, quousque aliud a nobis super hoc specialiter receperitis in mandatis, immo ipsos et eorum bona custodiatis et defendatis a novitatibus, iniuriis et violentiis quibuscumque, non enim intendimus nec volumus ad ipsos aliquas novitates extendi. Actum Parisius in vigilia festi beatorum Petri et Pauli apostolorum anno domini m^o cc^o nonagesimo quinto. (*28 June 1295*)

Appendix L.   COUNCIL OF THE PROVINCE OF ROUEN, SHORTLY BEFORE 3 MAY 1295
Evidence of the council held by the archbishop of Rouen, William of Flavacourt, is provided by the following royal acknowledgement of a grant.

1 .   **Royal acceptance of the grant of a biennial tenth**
Printed here from a copy in a cartulary of the cathedral church of Evreux: AD Eure, G122, item no. 398, fo. 132v (calendared in Inventaire Sommaire Eure, Série G, ed. Georges BOURBON (Evreux, 1886), pp. 56-88).

Philippus dei gratia Francie rex universis presentes litteras inspecturis salutem. Notum facimus nos recepisse oblationem quam pro subventione regni nostri prelati capitula abbates priores non exempti ac ceteri beneficiati provincie Rothomagensis nobis pro communi regni utilitate fecerunt in convocatione quam ad nostram fecit requisitionem dilectus et fidelis noster G[uillelmus] Rothomagensis archiepiscopus, videlicet per biennalem terminum ab unoquoque beneficiato dicte provincie qui hactenus decimam solvere consuevit levetur per ordinarios et nobis assignetur, dumtaxat quantum pro decima solvi consuetum est, sub modis et ordinatione qui secuntur. (i) Ordinaverunt namque quod dicta subventione durante omnes et singuli solventes decimam ac servi ecclesiarum et homines taliabiles de alto et basso sint ab omni impetitione et requesta alterius cuiuscumque subventionis immunes. (ii) Item, quod si simile onus vel equipollens in quotitate vel quantitate pro sede apostolica imponatur et levetur a personis predictis, dicta subventio cessabit omnino. (iii) Item, si pax reformetur, cessabit subsidium. (iv) Et si treuga iniatur inter reges, exactio differetur. (v) Item, quod si rex permittat quod duces comites seu barones petant et exigant ab aliquibus de personis predictis subsidium aliud non debitum, cessabit presens subventio quantum ad illas personas. (vi) Item, quod nullus prelatus ad armorum subsidium compellatur vel molestetur subventione durante, nisi necessitas forsitan quod absit urgeat, quo casu prelati facient quod debebunt. Que omnia grantanter (*sic*) acceptantes consentimus et volumus per concessionem nobis factam ex gratia speciali et liberalitate huiusmodi nullum ecclesiis ecclesiasticisve personis predictis inposterum preiudicium generetur, nec novum ius nobis in aliquo acquiratur. In quorum testimonium presentibus nostrum fecimus apponi sigillum. Actum Paris' die martis in festo inventionis Sancte Crucis anno domini m^o cc^o nonagesimo quinto. (*3 May 1295*)

INDEX OF MANUSCRIPTS

GENERAL INDEX